Don't Stop the Music

Finding the Joy in Caregiving

Nancy Weckwerth

Copyright © 2015 Nancy Weckwerth.

All rights reserved. No part of this book may be used or reproduced by any means, graphic, electronic, or mechanical, including photocopying, recording, taping or by any information storage retrieval system without the written permission of the author except in the case of brief quotations embodied in critical articles and reviews.

Balboa Press books may be ordered through booksellers or by contacting:

Balboa Press
A Division of Hay House
1663 Liberty Drive
Bloomington, IN 47403
www.balboapress.com
1 (877) 407-4847

Because of the dynamic nature of the Internet, any web addresses or links contained in this book may have changed since publication and may no longer be valid. The views expressed in this work are solely those of the author and do not necessarily reflect the views of the publisher, and the publisher hereby disclaims any responsibility for them.

The author of this book does not dispense medical advice or prescribe the use of any technique as a form of treatment for physical, emotional, or medical problems without the advice of a physician, either directly or indirectly. The intent of the author is only to offer information of a general nature to help you in your quest for emotional and spiritual well-being. In the event you use any of the information in this book for yourself, which is your constitutional right, the author and the publisher assume no responsibility for your actions.

Any people depicted in stock imagery provided by Thinkstock are models, and such images are being used for illustrative purposes only.
Certain stock imagery © Thinkstock.

Print information available on the last page.

ISBN: 978-1-5043-4465-4 (sc)
ISBN: 978-1-5043-4467-8 (hc)
ISBN: 978-1-5043-4466-1 (e)

Library of Congress Control Number: 2015918573

Balboa Press rev. date: 12/31/2015

Dedication

This book is gratefully dedicated to the Musicians of the "Professional Musicians, Local 47", in Los Angeles.

Their sincere and heartfelt desire to assist John with his recovery resulted in a fundraiser. This incredible event raised the funds that paid for John's private therapists for over two years. John would not be where he is today without their generosity. John and I are extremely and forever grateful for our professional musician colleagues.

Life is Transformed

*As we embrace the Tao,
our life becomes transformed.
Everyone around us feels the difference
and becomes more confident
amid the many issues
and concerns.*

*Nothing escapes our notice,
and we fully experience every moment.
Our caregiving transforms itself
into a time of wonder
and adventure.*

*How do we embrace the Tao?
By holding ourselves with great tenderness.*

From the book The Caregiver's Tao Te Ching. Copyright © 2011 by William and Nancy Martin. Reprinted with permission of New World Library, Novato, CA. www.newworldlibrary.com.

Foreword by Dr. Engel

He who saves a life, saves a universe. Nancy has saved one universe while preserving her own.

I first met John and Nancy in connection with a medical visit. His significant history consisted of a major stroke with a slow but unusually good recovery. In the initial episode he experienced one sided paralysis plus a neurological condition known as Broca's Aphasia. In this condition he could understand speech but had minimal ability to express his thoughts in decipherable words. As consistent with the standards of the time, a speech therapist had predicted that even with therapy he would never have a vocabulary of more than one-hundred and fifty words.

On examination John had the use of only one arm. However, he walked with a natural gait, had a surprisingly good vocabulary – and was consistently cheerful. The question posed itself: how did his remarkable recovery come about?

The answer to this question starts with the nature of John and Nancy's robust and honest partnership.

The required elements:

- Mutual attraction: difficult to predict, but something that will persist and grow if the other requirements are met.

- Friendship: this focused around their professional roles – but grew and became broader based over time.

- Mutual respect: this is the most important.

- A partnership: based on shared goals and values. This has been a central element in John's recovery. To understand this role it is necessary to focus on their identity as musicians and the neurological nature of Broca's Aphasia.

From childhood through adolescence there are continuous and major microscopic changes in the brain. There is a proliferation of neurons (nerve cells) each of which can be understood as a tiny microprocessor. Eventually they total about one-hundred billion. There are multiple connections between these cells. During childhood and adolescence there is a simultaneous massive selective proliferation and pruning of both neurons and connections.

This continues through life – but slows down greatly in the twenties. Mental activity and performances of complicated tasks affect it greatly. Intense study of music is the best example. If one is not qualified as a concert pianist at age twenty, it is almost impossible to achieve.

In Broca's Aphasia the major damage is to the connections between the neurons. In the recovery process these connections proliferate selectively [as if they were a child again]. It is strongly guided by the same processes that produce a concert musician.

In their successful collaboration Nancy contributed drive, encouragement, and a refusal to settle for minor victories. John's contribution was powered by a sunny disposition, his training, and basic identity as a musician. All these were imbedded in their full partnership.

Beyond telling John and Nancy's story the work is a valuable resource for any caregiver. In addition to the extensive factual material I would strongly recommend channeling Nancy's development as a ferocious patient advocate. With today's medical system, polite acquiescence is not an option.

A word of warning:

The modern recipe for a non-fiction best seller consists of a simple concept that can be expressed in one to three sentences surrounded by a cloud of anecdotes with variable relevance. Nancy's book expands upon the simplicity. It is completely real, well thought out, and requires work on the part of the reader. This book is well worth the effort.

As a final request to John and Nancy, I would ask that they revisit their plan of forming a special ensemble of musicians with both a classical and jazz experience (perhaps including themselves.)

It is never too late to revisit old dreams.

Eli Engel, M.D., Ph.D.

Foreword by Dr. Peterson

Just think about this—*Twenty-five years as the Primary Caregiver* for one's partner who has had a massive stroke! How does one cope? Author Nancy Weckwerth and her partner John Swan were in the midst of impressive, promising careers as talented musicians and entrepreneurs in the music industry. Then everything changed abruptly in 1991 with John's massive stroke. A life very different began for Nancy as Primary Caregiver and John as a person with a significant disability with an unknown future regarding his recovery.

How does one deal with the profound change this imposes upon life that was planned, a life-style that was dreamed of, and life accomplishments that were anticipated? *Don't Stop the Music* is an awesome, poignant book describing how Nancy and John have addressed the challenges of daily living and their happiness over the past twenty-five years since that life-changing day.

I had the good fortune of meeting Nancy Weckwerth and her partner John some sixteen years ago. That was approximately eight years following John's stroke. It was the beginning of a long-term professional and personal friendship. As a professional who has worked over forty-four years in the field of disability/special education and rehabilitation, the lives and daily challenges of individuals with disability and their families is a familiar arena for me.

Throughout our friendship, I have participated in many activities and projects with Nancy as well as with Nancy and John as a couple. We have shared ideas and long discussions. I have watched Nancy and John deal with daunting life issues that one might say are only for the strong-of-heart. I have always been impressed with the energy, positivism, determination, and creative ways by which Nancy tackles everything she does. So what she shares in this book is the kind of attitude, insight and wisdom that I have come to greatly respect over the years. Her perspective has been a constant source of inspiration in my own life. I have no doubt that other readers will find the same.

Just thinking about the daunting task that long-term caregiving can be, one might ask:

- How does one survive the never-ending responsibilities and demands upon one's life as a Caregiver (when no clear end may be in sight)?

- How does one resolve the endless stream of issues, problems, and challenges in this unfamiliar arena (for which no one is ever prepared) and which require continual problem-solving with creative solutions?

- How can one's own health and well-being be sustained given the stress, fatigue, and oftentimes overwhelming caregiving tasks on top of on-going duties of daily living (especially if the Caregiver <u>also</u> is sole wage-earner, financial manager, and the only adult running the household)?

- How does one retain a meaningful quality of life and still pursue one's own needs and dreams? Must one's former life-style, former sources of enjoyment and self-fulfillment be abandoned?

- How can one still find joy, happiness, and value in life given this changed existence? How does one learn to thrive in new ways?

These are questions that individuals in key caregiving roles often ask themselves. Such caregivers represent a growing population in the U.S. (whether this be with a spouse, an aging parent, or child due to illness, injury resulting in disability and/or long term medical challenges). AARP (American Association of Retired Persons) reports some 34,000,000 unpaid caregivers provide care to someone age 18 or older because of major illness or disability. The Family Caregiving Alliance reports approximately 65,700,000 unpaid caregivers in the U.S. for children, youth, or adults with health or disabling conditions that require intensive, continual supports by a Caregiver. This accounts for approximately 29% of the U.S. population. Over 66% of these caregivers are women.

Strokes, of the severity that John experienced, are one of the major causes of disability in adults requiring extended caregiving by another. No doubt, anyone assuming this important role for a loved one understands the profound responsibility and life changes that such events bring to both caregiver and the person requiring care.

<u>*Don't Stop the Music: Finding the Joy in Caregiving*</u> is an appropriate title for this retrospective perspective of Weckwerth's experiences as Primary Caregiver for her partner John. Looking back over those twenty-five years, the author vividly shares the meaning and ultimate resulting beauty of what was happening to her and John. She is able to see that challenging period as an opportunity given to her and John to step outside of themselves to become better, perhaps different people than they once imagined. They have changed—making a significant *"Paradigm Shift"* (a concept she explains in the book) in who they were/are and how they live in ways that Weckwerth describes as... "something more beautiful."

They are *still* learning. They are *still* changing and growing. So how have Nancy and John done this? What has fueled their extraordinary journey to arrive at such a place? This is the unique quality about this fascinating book. Its content goes beyond the story of John's progress toward recovery, the caregiving process, and life after stroke. From the viewpoint of Caregiver, Weckwerth offers a description of her insights and lessons learned as John's Caregiver along with her evolving philosophy about life's challenges.

Weckwerth's story and the wisdom gained/lessons learned holds clues for all of us as to how one can proceed with a positive, adaptive attitude through life when overwhelming challenges and unexpected life-changing events come upon us. No doubt, the rich narrative about Nancy and John's journey will stimulate much reflection and new thinking for anyone reading this book.

The author emphasizes that she and John made a conscious decision to embrace a positive attitude. They made a clear choice to take action, not to dwell on the trauma or frustrations that can be so acute in the face of such life-changing conditions. They focused upon living in gratitude for the good things in life. These were undoubtedly some of the strategies Weckwerth describes that were key to their "survival."

Weckwerth's account is up-lifting and a source of hope for persons currently or previously in a caregiving role or for a person just seeking a meaningful source of inspiration. Our author's goal of inspiring others to find their own solutions to caregiving challenges (and not wallowing in despair or wearing the cloak of "victim") is at the heart of her account about the caregiving process she has experienced. This book will do it. It is a remarkable, must-read story!

Early in the Prologue of her book, Weckwerth states an important value she embraces in all aspects of life—a clue as to how she has coped and indeed thrived given the challenges over these past twenty-five years as John's primary caregiver. *She states:*

> *"It is actually easy to make the choice to have a great attitude and live in gratitude. All you have to do is want to do it that way... When you make the choices and are grateful for your own solutions, you are no longer a victim."*

Her final punch line to this statement is so powerful, so beautiful. But I will let you read on in the book to find that. It is a wonderful statement that will play music in your head just as Nancy and John are playing their music. They now live in new ways they never before imagined.

Nancy L. Peterson, Ph.D.
Professor Emerita
Department of Special Education
School of Education
University of Kansas

Introduction: About this book

LEGAL DISCLAIMER: In this book, all accounts of medical occurrences are in no way intended to substitute for professional medical diagnosis or treatment for anyone else. The author is not a medical professional and nothing stated can be relied upon as medically accurate or as a substitute for professional medical care. This is a narrative of events as perceived and in the sole opinion of the author. Many of the descriptions may be inaccurate medically for two reasons:

- They are told from the point of view and recollections of what the author was told by medical and other professionals. To be absolutely clear, the author is not a professional medical healthcare provider and is not giving professional advice whatsoever. If the reader intends to obtain professional advice, the reader shall seek the services of licensed professionals. Moreover, all accounts of events are based upon the author's opinion and shall not be interpreted to be statements of fact.

- Medical science has advanced greatly in the twenty five years since John's stroke. Things change: paradigms shift. It must be understood by the reader that the methods, procedures, standards, testing, diagnosis, prognosis, medical care and treatment, and all other similar medical terms as understood in the industry may be currently different than when described within this manuscript.

The intention of the author is to provide an example or sample of hypothetical situations that could or may occur and how one can find joy after having experienced the possible situation.

No statements contained in this manuscript shall be interpreted to be defamatory whatsoever. <u>All statements shall be interpreted to be the opinion of the author.</u> The First Amendment to the Constitution protects freedom of expression. Moreover, the italicized paragraphs are expressly the thoughts and opinions of the author, and are an example of what the author was thinking at that time. Statements of opinion are privileged speech and are not actionable as defamation. This manuscript taken within its whole context, and as based on the Totality of the Circumstances, shall be considered to be constitutionally privileged speech.

Furthermore, all characters in this manuscript, other than the subject character and the author, have been fictionalized. Any possibility of anyone being identified with a fictional character within this manuscript and/or any resemblance of the fictional characters to an actual person is purely accidental. In addition, any terms or epithets, including but not limited to the terms "Scrubs" and "White Coats" as used in this manuscript, are merely figurative descriptions and are used as a representation of the opinions and thoughts of the author, and absolutely shall not be considered to be literal, derogatory, malicious, or defamatory in any manner whatsoever.

Moreover, and alternatively, for matters in which are argued to be factual, such matters are of public concern and it is understood that such statements are not made with any malice whatsoever, and are therefore subject to the fair comment of the author as protected by the First Amendment freedom of expression.

By continuing to read this manuscript, the reader agrees and consents that all statements contained in this manuscript are the mere opinions of the author and are absolutely not defamatory statements of fact.

How to read this book:

The chapters are topical, not chronological. It is not necessary to read them in order. Each chapter's intent is to cover the lessons learned and solutions from the specific point of view of the topic of that chapter. Since they can be read separately, there is a small amount of redundant information within each chapter. Most chapters contain some reference to the date and nature of Dr. John Swan's Cerebral Vascular Accident (CVA) or stroke and it is clearly understood by the reader that all statements within this manuscript are the opinions of the author based on her own experience of caring for Dr. Swan.

The format of the book is that of anecdote and then either Lessons Learned as a result of the situation or suggestions for Solutions.

> Lessons Learned appear in grey boxes.

> Suggestions and external informational commentary appear boxed.

Highly intimate discussion of the author's personal opinions, feelings, and thoughts occur within many of the chapters. Those sections appear in an italics font.

About the Author and Subject:

The Author, Nancy L. Weckwerth, M.M., B.M.E., with a Certificate in Composition for the Music Industry, is the Caregiver and Life-Partner for Dr. John D. Swan, the subject of the book. John had a massive stroke, or Cerebral Vascular Accident (C.V.A.) on February 12, 1991. Nancy has been his sole Caregiver since that time.

Both Weckwerth and Swan were professional musicians for their careers up until the time of the stroke. Their careers included performing in symphony, opera, and ballet orchestras, recording studios, dance bands, touring orchestras, and numerous smaller brass and woodwind ensembles in Miami, Toronto, and the Los Angeles area. A multi-tour stint with the Mantovani Orchestra found Weckwerth and Swan touring together throughout the United States and Japan. Dr. Swan also had an extensive performing career in other cities before they met each other in Florida. Both the Author and Subject had long careers in the education field. They taught at many different levels, including University and College professorships.

Additional information about John's recording and music compositional career can be found in Appendix II.

About the Poetry:

The author is profoundly pleased to share with you, quoted poetry from William and Nancy Martin's book, The Caregiver's Tao Te Ching: Compassionate Caring for your Loved Ones and Yourself. These items appear at the end of nearly every chapter of the book. They are included because of the simplicity, beauty, and wisdom of the Tao as translated or illuminated by William and Nancy. They are experts in the Tao Te Ching and have created many other translations of the Tao for specific users.

Contents

Dedication v
Life is Transformed vii
Foreword by Dr. Engel ix
Foreword by Dr. Peterson xiii
Introduction: About this book xix
Prologue xxix

Chapter 1   Emergency! A Life Changing Event 1
Chapter 2   Paradigm Shift: Embracing Change 16
Chapter 3   Finding Balance between the Health
            Care System and Personal Well-Being ... 36
Chapter 4   Happy Accidents are Miracles and Gifts ... 57
Chapter 5   The Caregiver's Health 76
Chapter 6   The Survivor's Health 100
Chapter 7   The Long Road: Physical and
            Occupational Therapy 127
Chapter 8   Silent No More: Re-learning to Speak 146
Chapter 9   Socializing Again: The Joy of
            Forgiveness 165
Chapter 10 Re-creating the Joy of Travelling 177

Chapter 11 The Pro-Active Caregiver: Patient
           Advocacy 200
Chapter 12 Moving through Mourning 217
Chapter 13 Don't Stop the Music: An Incredible
           Sense of Purpose 235
Chapter 14 A Triumph of Spirit: A New Kind of
           Music 258

Epilogue: Don't Stop Your Music 281
Acknowledgements 285
Appendix I 289
Appendix II 297
Appendix III 311
Index 315
About the Cover 319
About the Author 320

John D. Swan, DMA (Doctor of Musical Arts)

☙

**Dr. Swan had a massive stroke
on February 12, 1991.**

Prologue

I remember the precise moment when I knew I was in love with John. Like a dew drop that slips off a leaf and splashes to the rose petal below it, itself a cascade of rainbows falling through the misty air, love saturated my consciousness at our first kiss. It was a surprise! We had been friends and musical colleagues for years. The occasion of this event was after a lovely lunch together in a home I had just rented. I had invited John over for lunch to look at the house. He needed a place to live since he had just separated from his previous wife. I made a salad and a quiche. To say "thanks for the lunch", and "yes" I will take the other bedroom and rent it from you, he leaned over and kissed me. That moment is now frozen in time for both of us. In that instant, our world changed forever, the first of many life changing events.

Some things in life we choose and some things we do not. The first-kiss fireworks that burst for both of us were something we did not choose. In this case, the splendor of our love arrived after something we did not choose. How miraculously lucky we were!

We make many choices each day of our lives. We choose the item on the menu at a restaurant, or we choose to attend an opera performance. We are also bludgeoned with many things we do not choose each day. We did not choose for him to have a massive stroke in the prime of his career at the age of fifty-three. Years later, John and I did not choose to leave the "Batman" movie and find our car stolen from the multi-level parking lot at the theater, either.

Attitude, which tempers our many choices in life, comes most prominently into play as to how we approach the challenging things we do not choose. Challenges we do not choose provide the biggest choice of all. We can choose to deal with them well, or we can choose to deal with them poorly. So in essence, we do always have a choice. It is the choice of an attitude that allows for a positive response to all situations. Most often, we can discover that attitude by knowing it is founded in gratitude. A life affirming "thank you" for the lesson learned.

> This book is about learning to always choose to "deal with it well". It is about experiencing the joy of knowing that you did it well. At the end of every moment in our lives, there is joy, no matter what occurred during that moment if one allows the joy. Choose to live in that joyous moment. Allow your attitude to define your choice. There is joy and peace in that choice if you heed the message it brings. That message is to bravely meet the challenge.

> John and I accepted the challenge of his stroke from the perspective of our love, dealt with it well, and allowed it to change our lives as our paradigm shifted. If we could learn peace and joy from our circumstances, so can anyone who chooses to learn how.

ಌ

We have all known "victims". Those are the people we know who continually have the attitude of "why did this happen to me?", or "I'm the low person on the totem pole, the one that gets kicked in the shins", or (and this is my favorite) "I have **always been** the person who comes in last". Reality check: the victim mentality always brings the result that the victim expects. It is called the Law of Attraction in that we attract the energy that we put out, or that we expect. The irony in the choice to be the victim is that when one holds on to that choice, that is exactly what the Universe sends back. It is about assuming someone or something else is at fault. In the victim's mind it is certainly not their fault. Until they learn the lesson that they have chosen this attitude, the universe will continue to send them the same lesson, over, and over, and over again. It is their choice—to learn, or not to learn.

Victims also want someone else to take responsibility for them. In fact, many victims expect someone else to take responsibility for them. When their expectations are not met, they choose to be the victim again by wailing, "See, it was someone else's fault and it happened to me again!" It becomes a vicious circle.

This victim mentality is a learned attitude. Most of us began to learn this mentality as children. As an infant, we were unable to take responsibility for ourselves. Our parents took care of us. They fed us, changed us, and comforted us when we were unhappy. They did this out of love. We assumed that our parents would always be there for us because that is what we knew. We truly were helpless.

As we grew from an infant into a child, a good parent or teacher encouraged us to accept responsibility for ourselves and our decisions about ourselves. If we had a disagreement with a sibling, a good parent would encourage us to sort out the differences among ourselves and accept the responsibility for our choices. Responsibility prepares the child for adulthood.

Throughout life, great teachers guide us in the direction of personal accountability. They teach us to learn the source of an issue and then the teacher holds us accountable for our own success. Here is the most important lesson. Accountability is the solution that allows victimhood to vanish. Gradually we left childhood behind. With great role models and with a lot of practice, we learned how to make better choices that shaped our attitude about life in a positive manner. If we paid attention to the lessons, we learned to let go of the victim mentality and grow beyond it. Maturity means that we have accepted responsibility for ourselves and we hold ourselves accountable for success. We learn to sing our own song, one sweet melody at a time.

Herein lies the formula for joy, when we choose to take care of ourselves in all ways, we are no longer victims. A mature attitude eliminates the need to be a victim. Once we are no longer victims, the Universe opens up for us and allows our choices to be a part of what we manifest for ourselves. Our joy can escape from the caverns of adversity surrounding us, shine forth, and light up our world.

☙

> This book is about how John and I learned to choose not to be victims of his Cerebral Vascular Accident, or stroke, which occurred on February 12, 1991. We started by using a simple philosophy of attitude, choice, and gratitude. We made a conscious decision to have a positive attitude, we made choices to take action, and at all times remembered to live in gratitude for all things in our life.
>
> Throughout the book, these three concepts are mentioned relative to the specific examples that are revealed in each chapter.

It is actually easy to make the choice to have a great attitude and live in gratitude. All one has to do is want to do it that way. Make the choice to want it. Once the brain is open to the concept that one can make this choice, the Universe, Spirit, or God, (whatever one's preferred name for the divine is) allows our creative process to design our own solutions. All one has to do is choose to accept the responsibility to choose. When one makes the choices and we are grateful for our own solutions, we are no longer victims. This is the guiding principle of this book—step up on the podium, open the musical score, and hold the baton. Ask the divine for guidance on conducting.

> Essentially, here is the simple plan John and I followed after his stroke, and still follow today:
>
> - Analyze what our most immediate need is.
> - Say to our self, "How do I solve this immediate need?"
> - Once we come upon a plan, and here is the most important part: we **take action** on that plan.
> - At the end of each day, rejoice in gratitude that the events of the day unfolded in a way that creates joy in our life.
>
> This plan allowed us to erase victimhood from our choices. Because we made and still make positive choices, and take action, we live in gratitude and joy each day.

> **Examples of how we used this formula are included within each chapter.**

☙

It is important to remember that the solutions John and I found then, and still find everyday are probably not the same solutions that will be yours. We were not wealthy and our solutions involved finding ways to accomplish our goals with very little money. Our choice was to always find a solution. That way we moved beyond the problem and now live in joy.

Everyone's music is a different style. Find your own music, your own style and live it.

Welcome to our story.

Nothing We Cannot Face

Peace awaits us in the midst of trouble.
Hidden in all that we don't want
lies that which we most desire.
We sometimes feel alone and helpless,
but our deepest needs are being met.
There is nothing we need to avoid,
and nothing we cannot face.

Amid the chaos we realize
that we are strong and capable.

Nancy Weckwerth

*Living in uncertainty, we discover
that we can be content.
Even in the midst of loss we find
that the whole world belongs to us.*

"The Caregiver's Tao Te Ching" by William and Nancy Martin

Chapter 1

Emergency! A Life Changing Event

__The Phone Call__ hit me with a terror I had never felt before. My life-partner was being rushed to an ER. He had been at a rehearsal with a small group of jazz musicians and collapsed. They were working out the tunes for a new album. I truly don't even remember who called. It was February 12, 1991, two days before Valentine's Day. __The Phone Call__ told me it might be a stroke.

All I recall is a numbness settling on my brain like a dark gray fog. Clarity went out the door for a walk–a walk that lasted for many years.

Up until that moment, my life is that of a professional musician. John and I live in southern California. He is in demand as a trumpet player. I play (French) horn and piano. We are both composers. We have been publishing the music we write for about eight years now through our own company, Trombacor Music. We also compose whatever music is required for the next gig in the date book. For me, each day consists of a minimum of three hours of practicing my horn, some time writing music, performing, teaching, or working at a local retail store. I am happy in the certainty that this is and will be my life.

*When **The Phone Call** came, I was at my part-time job at the retail store. Since John had the car, I borrowed a car from a friend and left work to drive to the hospital.*

As I drove, my thoughts were spinning. I remember thinking at one point, this is the end. This phase of our life is over. I sensed it more than knew it. In one extremely brief moment, I was sorry we had not had a child to carry his incredible talent genes to another generation. I tossed out that thought with the bath water quicker than it had appeared. It never returned and I am more than grateful for that now.

During the drive, financial panic set in until I remembered that John now had health insurance. It was a mere ninety days since he had gotten it from my employers. I was immediately grateful and relieved.

The next panicked thought was sticking me like a voo-doo pin. How will I pay the rent in sixteen days if John's income from gigs is gone? What about the child support payments for his son living very far away? Food, gas, phone bills, car insurance? A million pins were sticking me. I was quivering and trying to drive.

*I do not remember the drive, only the voo-doo pins. And the **dark gray fog**.*

Looking back on that drive now, it is interesting that I was not thinking about John's condition. Since

I knew nothing more than it "might be a stroke", and I knew nothing about strokes, I did not have enough information to think about that. All of the other emotions and thoughts about security are the ones that leapt into my head. Suddenly I was out of control of my thoughts. I needed to control the car.

> **LESSONS LEARNED**
>
> The human brain spins its own web of emotions that are not in our control.
>
> In an emergency, the human brain retreats to its most basic of emotions: fear. Along with that comes the need for security.
>
> There is no shame in what one feels in an emergency. Knowing that whatever one feels at that moment is exactly what is right for that moment, frees one to deal with what needs immediate attention.

CR

I really dislike parking lots. My preference is to park away from other cars to avoid dings in my doors. Then I usually forget to notice where I park the car relative to where I'm going. It is still February 12. The dark gray fog is hanging over my head. I must remember where I have parked the car, the one I've borrowed from a friend.

John is in this very scary place: a hospital emergency room. Running on instinct, I feel myself moving into "support" mode. I must be cheerful and helpful. I must disguise my fear for John's sake.

*Ah, that's what this cloud is, it's **Fear**.*

*So it is **Fear** that is creeping in and settling in my psyche. I'm cold. **Fear** is cold. It's cold in this emergency room. Why are hospitals always so cold? Isn't there enough to be uncomfortable with and afraid of without adding bone-chilling cold to the equation? I'm not amused by my own half-hearted attempt at humor.*

When I find John he is relieved to see me. His bed is in an empty black space that must be a large room. My focus is on him like a spotlight on a performing stage. Everything else is swallowed up in the blackness that exists outside of the spotlight. People in scrubs meander into the light every now and then and interrupt our conversation. We chatted, I guess. I have no recollection of what we said to one another. Little did I know that these were the last real conversations I would ever have with him.

*The **Scrubs** are waiting for **The Phone Call** from the insurance company telling them that he is covered and they can treat him. Up until this point, there has been no treatment, merely observation, I speculate. I don't know what time it is, or how long we have been waiting for **The Phone Call**, or even what "treatment" means at this time.*

While I'm standing in the spotlight beside his bed, John suddenly takes his left hand and lifts up his right hand and arm. While saying "look!" he releases the right arm and it falls sickeningly to the bed. Neither of us knew what that meant at the time. It is probably a good thing we did not know because **Fear** *would have caused me to faint.*

He was having another stroke. This second event paralyzed his right arm immediately. His right leg was gone, too, but we didn't know it yet.

I vaguely remember being in an adjoining hallway with some cabinets and a phone on the counter. All of a sudden it rings and the **Scrubs** *pick it up. They tell me it's* **The Phone Call** *and they can now treat John. Relief spreads through me in little waves. I want to believe it is big waves but I don't dare risk letting go of the dark* **Fear** *I'm clutching in my soul. I discover John has been whisked away from my spotlight. My thinking is so unlike my normal self.* **The Cloud-Fog** *is back in force because the spotlight is gone. Everything is so empty.*

Later, after finding John in a more private room, not the emergency room, the **Scrubs** *tell me they are trying to stabilize him and keep his heart and blood pressure normalized. He is on a monitor that sets off an annoying alarm every time he is in danger. We now know it is definitely a stroke or Cerebral Vascular Accident. He's had two.*

*I opt to sleep in a chair next to his bed overnight. His heart monitor alarm goes off and wakes me every hour or so. The **Fear Cloud** is becoming thicker. I run down to the nurse's station repeatedly to tell them the alarm is going off. In my opinion, the **Scrubs** there give me the distinct impression that they cannot be bothered with coming to John's room yet again to turn off the poisonous noise spewing from the machines connected to John.*

This continues for more hours than I can track in my sleepless haze. There are far too many "whys" stomping through my brain leaving sucking noises in the muck.

Morning looms, I think, in this windowless room on February 13. It must be morning because there is the noise in the hallways of more activity. John awakens for a moment every now and then. I don't know if he knows where he is, or who I am.

*At one point, the **Scrubs** enter and tell me I may as well go home and get some real sleep. Apparently John will sleep for many more hours and there is nothing I can do. I will need my rest.*

*I must have found the car and driven home, but I don't remember any of it. Only the **Fear Cloud** that followed me home.*

☙

It was Valentine's Day: the morning of February 14, 1991. I had rustled through John's dresser at home looking for clothing for him and discovered a brand new woman's blue sweater in one drawer. I realized that it was his Valentine's present for me. I decided to wear it. After having spent the rest of the previous day making arrangements with a friend to drive me to our car, I drove to the hospital. The ever-present **Fear Cloud** was still with me. It had now settled into a large knot in my stomach. Breathing was challenging because my chest was so tight. At least I was warm in my new sweater.

When I arrived in his room, an awake John could not greet me because his speech was completely gone. Another shock. Overnight his brain had continued to swell from the stroke damage, and he was unable to speak. More and more of "John" had been whisked away during the night.

He saw the blue sweater and reached for me with his now only working arm, his left. He grabbed my arm and tugged on the sweater with the hint of a smile. Facial muscles were not working right either. That hint though, told me that he was still there, inside the cocoon of brain damage. I sputtered some words of comfort and he turned away from me towards the wall, refusing to be a part of life.

A moment of pure divine inspiration came to me and I said "John, this did not just happen to you, it happened to us. We have two choices here, we can do this well, or we can do this poorly. You and I will choose to do it well." In that moment, John made a choice. He turned back to me and with his eyes, he told me "Yes". We had made a pact. We became a different team. We had always been a team as musicians, now we had unwittingly become a team for "rehabilitation from stroke" even though that entire term was unknown to us at that time.

It is impossible to describe the **POWER** we both felt, together, at that moment. **The Cloud** was starting to dissipate.

Later that day John was moved to yet another room. This one was private. A **White Coat** finally arrived to talk to me. It was my first conversation with him. I asked him what a stroke was, because I really didn't know. I was so naïve. He explained what it was and told me that John would not be able to work for at least two years, and probably never again.

Anything else he said to me went unheard after that announcement. When he left the room, I literally crawled on the floor and hid under John's bed and sobbed. John slept through all of this with the head end of the hospital bed raised. I don't know how long I sat on the floor, in my private space of collapse. Eventually, I crawled out from under the bed and faced **The Cloud** from a position of strength. I had to. There was no one else to help. John and I were alone in this new and unfamiliar path.

John remained in the first hospital until he was fully stable. Then I was told he would be moved to a hospital closer to our home that was on our insurance plan. On the appointed day, I waited at the second hospital for him to arrive. I waited several hours, or at least what seemed like several hours to me. Time had become a non-entity for me. I was always either waiting or moving to the next situation to wait. **The Cloud-Fog** was never gone. It just gave me moments of respite, only to return when I was not looking.

I think it was either the fifth or sixth day after the stroke when John was moved to the second hospital. I only remember seeing him come down the hall on a gurney and saying to the driver, **"This one belongs to me!"**

The days were now a blurry haze within **The Cloud-Fog**. I had gone back to work after three days off. Now I needed the money from my barely-above-minimum-wage part-time job. Gratefully, I was the manager of the department in which I worked. The first thing I did was to give myself a full thirty-five-hour work week to increase my income. They needed me there more, anyway, so it was a win-win. I had flipped into "solution" mode to solve our financial concerns.

Well, **my** concerns. I quickly realized that John was no longer a part of the financial team as an asset earner in our household. He was now a complete financial liability. The full realization of this fact was an explosion of dirty-bomb capacity on my time and awareness.

All the "whys" of the previous days since the curtain dropped had now turned into "hows". My thoughts revolved around "How was I going to provide the income? How was I going to find the time to hold down a full time job?

How was I going to support him emotionally, physically, psychologically? How was I going to get him back to normal?" I actually believed normal was still possible.

At this point, I added another layer of duty to my roster. John refused to eat hospital food at the second hospital as he had at the first. So, I cooked his food each evening, and brought it into the hospital for him each morning when I visited at 7:00 a.m. The kinder **Scrubs** at this hospital were happy to refrigerate it and heat it for him at noon. In the evening after work, I went back to the hospital to visit and bring another meal for him.

It never even occurred to me at this time that I was heading down a path of no return. That path was one of permanent Caregiver to a person with a handicap. Each new self-assigned task was assumed without even a twinge of anger or resentment. There was no time to be angry or resentful. It just "had to be done", so I did it. I added layer upon layer to my schedule. I was in shock. It was months before the shock began to dissipate and I allowed the anger and resentment to drop in for a long visit.

LESSONS LEARNED

Decisions made along the journey are always made with the information one has at the moment.

Also, who one is as a person and one's relationship with the Survivor will determine what one does or does not do.

> Ultimately, when anger and resentment set in, know it could not have been done any differently at that time. Awareness of the fact that one acted with the information one had at the moment will help the anger and resentment dissipate.

After a week or ten blurry days of a regular hospital stay with minimal rehabilitation, John's insurance moved him to the rehabilitation unit. Since this unit had a reputation as being one of the finer rehab units in Southern California, I was delighted. I felt that now he would begin making some real progress.

On a daily basis, John received speech, occupational, and physical therapy. **The Phone Calls** at my work became a ritual. "Nancy, Line 1" became my new dreaded words as they bellowed over the retail store intercom system. Especially memorable were the reports from the speech therapist. Her statement, "John will never speak more than 150 words" still echoes in my nightmares. When I heard that, I did nearly crawl behind the counter in the store and hide again. This was not my definition of the "normal" to which John would return. I decided that somehow John and I would prove this therapist wrong. The seesaw ride for me from "pronouncement to determination" to "new pronouncement to further resolve" was now making me dizzy within **The Cloud-Fog**.

The Phone Calls continued ad infinitum as they came almost daily, and often more than once in a day.

The telephone cord began to feel like a hangman's noose to me.

After two weeks in the rehab unit, the next life-shattering announcement from the **White Coats** was that there may be a cheaper way to do this. Something inside me snatched those words and etched them on my forehead, even though I had no idea what they meant at the time.

It became clear a few days later when **The Phone Call** came that John was being moved in an hour, to a Skilled Nursing Facility, abbreviated, SNF.

AN HOUR?

They had to be kidding. I was told to get there to register him. I felt as if I was swimming upstream in icy unknown waters again. The "whys" returned. "Why are they taking him away from this wonderful hospital. Why are they placing "normal" further from his and my reach?"

I was so alone. I could barely breathe with the rope squeezing my chest.

I now know that this was only the beginning of many ridiculously short notices for massive changes in the system in which John was hopelessly entangled.

In my effort to remain as cheerful and supportive as possible in front of John, I arrived at the SNF with a smile on my face and went to the reception desk. After an introduction there, the young gal at the desk took out her clipboard and began questioning me. When I quickly answered her third query and gave his social security number, she asked "How do you know that so quickly?" I was shocked by her comment. Why would I not know my life-partner's social security number, especially since I had had to repeat it about four thousand five hundred and seventy-six times since the curtain fell?

The next question she asked was **"What funeral home will you be using?"** I nearly vomited. The abject cruelty of that question rankles me to this day. I thought torture chambers were illegal in America. Fortunately, I was leaning with my elbows on the counter. My knees went weak and had I not been leaning on the counter, I would have fallen to the floor. In what Universe is that the next question after name, address, and social security number? Shouldn't they first ask why the patient was being admitted? Are there no standards or training for these workers that teach them compassion?

"Does this emotional roller-coaster that I'm on ever slow down? Can I get off this ride?" These were my thoughts. The ever present **Cloud-Fog** was exceptionally dark on this day.

All of this intense emotional upheaval continued for the next thirty days. I felt like a child's top being spun around and around at a dizzying pace. My schedule book became a useless entity in my purse because all of the entries had so many changes that it looked like a redacted spy document. The moment I thought or felt *that some kind of stability was returning to my daily schedule, another **Phone Call** would come and the world would change again.*

*I realized that this turmoil had become so ingrained in my days that it was starting to bother me less. Confusion had become the norm. I had reached a point in my life where **The Cloud-Fog** just belonged. It was the new normal.*

Even emergencies were not unexpected. Work went forward, each day the sun rose, and each night I fell exhausted into my bed. That didn't mean that I slept when I went to bed, it just meant that I was horizontal for a few hours. Sleep began to elude me as my brain whirl-winded through the tasks for the next day, and the next.

*Looking back, I now know that all of these behaviors and feelings on my part are the norm for Caregivers. I wish that I had known the word Caregiver. I wish that someone would have mentioned that word. Funny thing is, in **1991** there was precious little reading material on the career of Caregiver. I guess knowing the word would not have made a difference then anyway, because I did not have time to read.*

As I reflect on all of this now, the reality of my situation that I was totally and completely on my own, finally entered into my consciousness: I had become a Caregiver.

You Remain

*Don't waste your time trying to understand
why things are as they are.
Don't believe all the stories you are told
about what's important
and not important.
Don't get stirred up by wanting this
and avoiding that.*

*You are a plain and simple being,
an expression of the Tao.
Even when everything you thought secure
is slipping out from under you,
you remain.*

"The Caregiver's Tao Te Ching" by William and Nancy Martin

Chapter 2
Paradigm Shift: Embracing Change

Picture yourself sitting in a moderately full subway car. At a stop, a man enters with two young children. He sits down, but the wiggling children are not cooperating with his request to sit. They start charging about in the car, kicking over backpacks, luggage, and packages on the floor. They begin to scream and yell. The other passengers, you included, are becoming annoyed with the unsavory and rude behavior of these children. The father does nothing to control his stampeding herd. He seems unaware of their effect on others. You decide to see if you may assist and walk over to the father and say, "Excuse me sir, but your children are running around all over the car and I am concerned for their safety." With a rather dazed look in eyes, the father seems to snap back to the present, and after a short pause to assimilate what you have said, haltingly replies, "Oh, I'm sorry, I wasn't aware. We just came from the hospital where their mother just died. I g-guess we're all in shock."

Think about your reaction to the event. What were your thoughts as the children were running around in the subway car? What are your thoughts now that you know the background of the family's recent event? Did your concept of the situation CHANGE as a result of your new knowledge of the situation? Most likely you now feel compassion for the family and your irritation at the children subsides. This change in your concept is called a Paradigm Shift. Because of new knowledge about the situation, your thoughts and reactions have shifted to a new arena. More importantly, you cannot go back to your previous concept: new knowledge has forever changed the parameters of the situation.

◅◦▻

When I heard this allegory, it helped me realize what had happened to John and me as a result of his stroke. Our entire life paradigm had shifted. This story helped me realize that there was a new definition to who we were. It helped me define and arrange my emotions regarding the tumultuous changes we were forced to accept in our lives. And now, instead of thinking in terms of "force" I learned that as time passed and as we moved into "accepting" all the lifestyle alterations we made to accommodate John's ability changes, the miracle in our story occurred. Because we changed how we lived, it became easier to make more changes, and the more we changed, the easier it became.

This method of accepting challenges and discovering a new way is how we have been able to make the shift to joy in our new life. Over the many years of our journey we have embraced the change instead of holding on to the past ways of doing things. This ability to change and shift was not immediate, but blossomed over time. Now, our many paradigm shifts have created the joy in our lives.

Following are several anecdotes that reveal how we changed how we thought, what we did, and thereby were able to move into a more love-based status spiritually regarding our extreme change in lifestyle. This chapter discusses some of the long term changes made in our lifestyle that have been necessary to upgrade the quality of life for the Survivor and for the Caregiver.

All of the things I will discuss in this chapter may be obvious to you or they may not. As I have gone through life attending seminar after seminar in my field, my policy has always been, if I learn one new thing from this seminar, then it has been worth my time. I hope you, as a reader, will find at least one Solution that is useful to you from reading this chapter.

The secret is to allow change. It is about attitude. Whenever an old method of doing a particular thing or an old habit no longer serves the best interests or "highest good" of the participants, a different or better way must be discovered.

There are no rules that say you have to do anything a particular way other than the rules in your own head. The rules in your head are merely thoughts and thoughts can be changed. Of course one must use good judgment to maintain safety and encourage personal growth when considering change. It is not acceptable to go backward in methods or to ignore safety considerations.

ɔ҄

There are two categories of changes we made and are still making as new challenges arise. Simple changes were made to our home, car, and yard, such as adding wheelchair ramps to assist with the physical aspect of his partial paralysis. More importantly, there are two complex or profound changes that have been made to accommodate both of our emotional and spiritual paradigm shifts.

Embracing simple changes

Early on, John was able to prepare simple meals on the stove by heating canned goods, or using frozen foods in the microwave. Since he had only one functional arm and hand, his left, there were many things that required altering. For example, John could not use a can opener. That appliance requires two hands. One hand holds the tin can, and the other pushes down on the lever device that opens the can. Therefore, any canned goods had to be opened by me in advance, placed in a covered pan with a handle, and refrigerated. Then when John was ready to eat, he could take the pan out of the refrigerator and put it on the stove. This worked only when it was a very short distance from the refrigerator to the stove because he could not use his cane to walk and hold the pan at the same time. As John aged, his walking deteriorated to where he could only walk with a cane. Cooking canned goods by him, by himself, using this method was no longer an option.

I have always monitored his safety behaviors, but especially those in the kitchen. Most importantly I made sure he always remembered to turn the stove off when he was done. This constant vigilance on safety issues has become very wearing on me. For over twenty-five years I have felt like I was monitoring a four to six year old child, all day, every day. This never goes away so I have learned to let go of my angst about it. Once I let go, it became much easier for me to monitor him. I am deeply grateful that most of his safety consciousness was intact regarding cooking.

Microwave cooking has challenges for John, too. His cognitive ability regarding not using any metal in the microwave has never returned. Even after years of explaining "only plastic" or "no metal", he cannot grasp it conceptually. To solve the problem, I prep all food items that he will microwave, making sure they are in microwave safe containers. Then I put a sticky note on the item in the refrigerator with a timer amount for them to be cooked. 15 seconds, 2 minutes, or whatever is required. With that one simple instruction, he can use the microwave.

In addition, John cannot read the instructions on the back of a frozen meal and follow them. This is part of the brain damage he experienced during the stroke. By the time he reads the first step of the instruction and tries to do it, when he goes back to the instructions to find the next step, he cannot remember what he just read and did previously. He gets lost. Confusion sets in. He can only follow one simple instruction.

Another kitchen safety lesson learned was to switch all eating dishes and drinking vessels to plastic or melamine. It only took a few broken dishes with their potential for bloody cuts for me to realize our lovely dinner sets could only be used by me. I simply put the china dishes in a cupboard that he could not reach and put all the plastics right next to the microwave and stove for him. This sounds simple, but no amount of explaining or teaching regarding acceptable dishes sunk into his mental abyss. I just removed the temptation to use anything else because he was not able to judge what was safe in this arena.

Brain damage is interesting as there is no logic or consistency to what works in his mind. It was a learning process for me to observe his process and for me to change. It became necessary to adapt my work patterns around what worked and what did not work for him. I learned to bend and change how I did things because he could not.

Here is another facet of John's brain damage that requires simple but important changes on my part. John is unable to make appropriate decisions for seasonal adjustments of clothing. No amount of explaining that it is summer, it is really hot, so therefore it is not a good idea to wear sweatpants, sweaters, or put blankets on his lap on the couch ever causes him to dress or act appropriately. It is actually dangerous for stroke victims, according to one of his doctors. He is unaware that he is hot, does not know to keep himself hydrated with the beverages I keep in front of him, and his brain shuts down from overheating. He gets really goofy and he looks like a deer in the headlights. He loses all awareness of how he feels and what is going on. Therefore he does not know what he could do to help himself. He can actually get dehydrated and faint.

To solve this issue, each season I simply reorganize his closet and drawers to put only appropriate clothing in his reach when he is dressing. In summer, I remove all the blanket throws from the couch and fold them into a storage location. I place all long sleeved shirts and long pants in an area of the closet he cannot reach. In winter, I bring back the blanket throws, his long pants, sweatpants, and I place sweaters within his reach. He seems to be very aware of when he is cold. He will put a blanket on his lap to keep warm in winter.

For the first five years after the stroke, John was not able to dial a phone. It was the same reason as following the directions on the back of frozen food packages; he cannot look at a phone number and dial it. His brain sees the first number, dials it, and then when he looks back at the number to be dialed, he has no idea what number is next for him to dial. There was another simple solution for us. Thank heaven for more advanced phone technology in that I can set up his phone with one touch pre-programmed dialing. All he has to do is read the name of the person he wants to call and push the number assigned to that name. Even this solution took five years for him to learn.

For the first twelve to fifteen years or so after the stroke, John took a daily walk part ways around the block to get some exercise. In order to make this happen, I installed handrails at all doors on the house that he would use. John has the use only of his left arm and left hand. His right arm and right hand are useless. Therefore he had to have a handrail on both sides of all stairs. When he walks up stairs, he steps up with his left leg and then, holding the railing with his left hand while holding the cane at the same time, he sort of swings his right leg up the step. When he goes down the steps, he must use the hand railing on the other side of the steps. It is also important to have steps with little or no "lip" between the tread and the riser so he does not catch the toe of his right foot on the lip and trip. That was actually one of the times that caused a dangerous fall for him when entering a friend's home. Fortunately he was not seriously injured, just a scrape on his knee from the bricks.

I am grateful that my father is a builder. He built new steps at the exterior doors in our home that John used most often. Dad built the steps with very low risers and no lip so John could easily go in and out of the house.

The bathroom changes have been very simple for us, too. A portable shower seat allows John to get into the bathtub as long as I assist with getting his legs into the tub. He cannot lift his right leg into a bathtub on his own. A handheld shower allows him to bathe himself. When we moved to the second home, there was a small corner shower stall in the bathroom off his practice studio. It was so small, and in such a small room that he could get into the shower, sit on the shower seat, bathe himself, and get out again without any help from me. The ultra-small room meant that if he slipped, there was nowhere for him to fall because he just ended up leaning on another wall. What a miracle this was for both of us! He got to maintain his dignity, and I was freed from the daily scheduling of his bath on top of my already overcrowded schedule.

Grab bars in showers and near toilets only work if they are on the side of the room that will accommodate their use with his left hand only. Until you have had to deal with someone with only one arm, these complications never occur to you. For John, we use them if they are appropriate.

Most of the other things discussed are based upon taking care of a person who is partially paralyzed and can now walk slightly, but whose balance is severely compromised. While standing, even with his cane, John tips over if you poke him lightly with a finger. This leaves him terrified all the time. His fear of falling is extreme. He has fallen many times, too. We have been lucky there have not been more injuries. For this reason, we use a wheelchair outside of the home. It is far too easy for someone in a crowd to bump him. He can fall over because he does not have the ability to correct a fall by moving a foot, or grabbing something for support. He just tips over.

Using a wheelchair creates its own set of challenges. Those challenges involve loading it in and out of vehicles, finding accessible ramps and the Caregiver's fatigue at doing both of those. Solving those issues is just a matter of practice: the more you do it, the more it becomes a part of your daily regime. Auto pilot kicks in.

In the twenty-five years since his stroke, John has worn out one wheelchair and is well on the way to doing the same with the second one he owns. At one point I tried getting a wheelchair through the government health insurance program, but they only rent-by-the-month to those who need them now. The government learned that when they bought wheelchairs, elderly people often needed them for only a very short time. These people would pass on, and a wheelchair was lost to the insurance system. They determined that rental-only was the less expensive way to handle wheel chairs for elderly people. I explored the rental option and learned that the only chairs that they rented were the heavy chrome metal chairs. Those chairs weigh about thirty-five to forty-five pounds. For me, lifting a thirty-five to forty-five pound chair in and out of a car six to eight times a day was not an option. The toll on my back was way too extreme.

The solution for us has been to buy his chair. His current one was purchased through private therapists who had a dealership for wheelchairs and other equipment for people with handicaps. They came to our home, measured John, and helped us select the best chair for us. Since John is quite short, we were able to get the largest child-size chair. This chair weighs in around sixteen pounds. This is a huge difference for me relative to my lifting it in and out of a vehicle. Changing how we thought about his equipment relative to its functionality for him and its effect on me has become critically important. We shifted our paradigm to include my health in the decision making process.

Another change we embraced regarding the wheelchair was in purchasing a car for us. When I went car shopping, I took the wheelchair along with me. The first thing I did was open the trunk of the prospective vehicle, and check the ease of getting a chair in the trunk. If it was not easy, or it did not fit, I moved to a different choice of car. Simple.

John fell out of bed while sleeping a couple of years ago. His cane was sitting next to the bed and he landed on it. His scream for me in the middle of the night woke me and sent me flying into his room. I found him lying on the floor, on top of his metal cane. The cane had lodged between the bed and a bookshelf and it was now bent in a curve. After questioning him, he did not remember falling, but woke up once he had been on the floor for a while. I do not know if he had knocked himself out or not. What I do know is that the folding cane would never fold or be useful for him again. I also found the huge bruise on his side where he had landed on it. Fortunately, he did not break any bones with this fall.

The first time he did this was the only time. It was a wake-up call for me. The next morning I got on the Internet and ordered a bedrail for him. It arrived in a week. This particular one fits all bed sizes from twin to king via a pair of straps that run from the bedrail to the opposite side of the bed under the mattress, and attach to the opposite frame. It is an ingenious device that folds down with a quick flip of two switches so I can change sheets. John told me the second night he used it, "safe". He now felt safe in his bed. Another simple change.

CR

Embracing complex changes

> **LESSONS LEARNED**
>
> I now know that all of the following challenges were layered on me, day after day, for a reason. They were the impetus for me to change. These were more complex changes because they involved psychological, emotional, and spiritual changes. They were often more subtle changes at the time, too. It is only in retrospect that I am aware of these slow, creeping changes. These changes were the major paradigm shifts that we made. They ultimately have become the new definition of who we are.
>
> It was my choice to accept the changes that were occurring or resist them.
>
> One of the many lessons I have learned along the way is that what we resist, persists. Things persist until we stop resisting and move into acceptance and finally gratitude.

I have made two major paradigm shifts throughout the years that are emotional and spiritual in nature. The explanation of these changes requires an anecdotal approach that reveals more of the story of the initial weeks and months after the stroke.

*As John is being moved to the Skilled Nursing Facility or SNF, about five weeks after his stroke, I am saturated with **fear**. I am choking on **fear**.*

*So far, we have been to the first hospital emergency room, shifted to acute care in that hospital, evacuated a few days later to the stabilized care unit of a hospital closer to our home, moved to the rehabilitation unit of that hospital, and then ripped from there with two hours' notice and shipped unceremoniously to the SNF. Each time John is moved, I have to start over again, learning the methods and rules of each location. This enormous amount of change is all within the time frame of less than thirty-five days. Each move, often miles apart, to a new room, a new hospital, a new set of nurses and doctors, catapults both of us into **fear** of the unknown again and again.*

My emotions are raw from the events of the previous thirty-five to forty days. I feel like all of these changes are being forced upon us for reasons unknown.

I actually feel like a pinball in a pinball machine, endlessly bouncing from bumper to bumper, struggling to not slide into the drain of the machine, only to be spring loaded and bounced back to the play table again. I am numb from all the changes.

*My sixth sense tells me that the arrival at the SNF is a definite downgrade in quality of care from everything prior. Most notably, my black **fog** of fear is definitely back, hovering over my head each day. All I want to do is stop, be still, and have time to reorganize my thoughts, emotions, and my schedule in order to accommodate the constant changes. I need to stop having to make so many decisions about our existence within the changes.*

The many changes in location and treatment style for John are so far away from the life we lived a mere thirty-five days ago. I'm exhausted.

*How can they keep doing this to us? Why aren't we a party to any of their decisions? There is no discussion with me, merely a **Phone Call** with "John is being moved today, in two hours, to such and such place. Be there to register for him." Click. What an infuriating sound.*

I feel as if they are treating John merely as a number on a file, spinning his life around dollar signs in their spreadsheets. It has nothing to do with who he is, how talented he is, what an amazing musician he is. Does not forty years as a top of the line career trumpet player count for simple decency in how he is treated? I am infuriated and insulted by this lack of respect for him and for us.

If I am the pinball, he is a flipper in the pinball machine: endlessly pushed back and forth without any clear objective and then having the hapless support pinball bounce away just as it is needed, again. We are mere pieces in a financial game for these people who are puppet-like fronts for "the company".

I have problems getting the doctors to talk to me. I have learned that all of the decisions are made by an Administrative Nurse in the Provider Group. Doctors can recommend, I believe, but the Administrative Nurse has the power of the purse. I get the distinct feeling that the doctors are not happy with the decisions made administratively so maybe that is why they avoid talking to me. Without information from the doctors, it is virtually impossible for me to make needed medical decisions. All I can do is base any decisions I make on the information I have.

> ## LESSON LEARNED: The First Shift
>
> My first major paradigm shift was deeply spiritual. It involved all the changes made in our lifestyle, our helplessness, and most importantly the resentment that all of these engendered because of who we were as individuals prior to the stroke.
>
> My first major shift was that I learned that none of these things has any significance at all. None of these changes, from the stroke forward has had any effect on who we really are. It has not affected our true self, that pure inner soul of our spirituality. These items were mere surface earthly experiences that have actually served us. They have helped us become aware of our true self. The initial resentment is gone. I am now deeply grateful that we had all those experiences.

At that point in my life, it was nearly twenty years before I would learn the concept of a love-based emotion or approach, as opposed to a fear-based emotional approach to everything. Had I known then, what I know now, my awareness of that knowledge would possibly have helped me make those paradigm shifts with less emotional toll on me. I learned about this concept from reading "A Return to Love" by Marianne Williamson.

A love-based emotion is one that is joyous, accepting, heartfelt, and in the best interest of all parties to the decision. A fear-based decision is one that is one-sided, benefitting only one party to the decision, reactionary, or you feel that it has been forced upon you. The trick for me was to learn to change fear-based decisions into love-based emotional reactions to decisions.

Here is an example of how I learned a valuable lesson on how to make that change.

When John and I moved from the second house to the smaller apartment in another city, we lost the option for him to bathe himself. Our new digs had a bathtub and he cannot get into a bathtub without my assistance. At first I started out helping him with his daily bath thinking, "I **have** to bathe John every day." The burden of that task was weighing heavily on me relative to scheduling, and just assuming the responsibility for taking care of him this way again was onerous. After a few weeks of this, I realized there may be an easier way for me. Instead of thinking "I have to bathe John" I changed and said to myself "I **get** to bathe John and provide a loving service to him." Immediately, the weight lifted from my shoulders. I freed myself. It was no longer difficult, it became an easy little bit of every day where we laugh and have fun together. Because I made the choice to change how I thought about the task at hand, I was able to make a paradigm shift to a love-based emotion and move into joy.

༺ཨོཾ༻

As the years passed, it became apparent to me that I had made an even bigger change. It was about who I was relative to making the decisions for us. The biggest paradigm shift of all for me was that I had to shift to sole decision maker, sole breadwinner, sole director of therapy, and general manager of the entire household. I had lost my partner. There was no more sharing of these duties with John. He was no longer able to be part of our previous team. I was alone, and it was lonely.

That loss has been the most difficult for me to accept.

> **LESSON LEARNED: The Second Shift**
>
> My acceptance of the shift to sole decision maker has changed another paradigm for me. This acceptance is my second major paradigm shift. My old paradigm was that we had to be a team to make decisions and my value was as part of the team. My new paradigm is that I am perfectly capable of making the decisions for us on my own. I sometimes run things by John, as a courtesy, but I know his brain damaged state does not allow him the reasoning skills required for major decision making. I limit his involvement to simple things.

> My new role, as major decision maker, now brings me great joy as I evolve into a more confident and loving being. This confidence is a result of experiencing the success of my decisions. The loving is a result of knowing that all my decisions were and are, made in the best interests of us as a team. They are made with love and the desire for the best quality of life possible for both of us. Even the occasional wrong decision is part of my shift.
>
> Any decision can be analyzed to see if it was made as a result of love-based emotions or intentions. In retrospect if a wrong decision was made, forgive your self-judgment and make a new decision to correct it.

This spiritual paradigm shift brings the most joy and contentment possible. It is spiritual because I know that my ability to make this shift is a gift from Spirit. I am no longer alone. With the help of Spirit, my team role has merely shifted. Along with it, I live in joy as a Caregiver.

A Part of All That Happens

These circumstances did not arise
to purposefully make us suffer.
They are not a plot
to keep us in a constant struggle,
to get us to wrest some peace from turmoil,

and finally triumph over our cruel fate.

*Our peace comes when we let go
and see the whole of life
instead of the tiny, separate parts.
Our triumph arrives when we become
a part of all that happens
rather than apart from it.*

"The Caregiver's Tao Te Ching" by William and Nancy Martin

Chapter 3

Finding Balance between the Health Care System and Personal Well-Being

> My personal definition of balance is this:
> Balance is the art of keeping all aspects of one's life on track, in a love-based emotional state, and therefore maintaining an attitude of gratitude.

When life challenges us beyond what we normally expect in our day to day routine, it is incredibly easy to feel out of balance, overwhelmed, frightened, and any other emotion based on fear. Finding and keeping balance is challenging when external forces cause unforeseen events to occur. When John had his stroke, I was on a tightrope from the first moment, trying to find balance between those two emotions. I was feeling love for John and fear for the future of our lives. I felt totally out of balance because I was reacting to a situation moment by moment that was occurring moment by moment. Most significantly, the challenges were imposed by external forces beyond my control.

The skill to maintain balance in such situations is one that can be developed providing one has the tools necessary to do so. Like any building project good tools are essential. Tools can come from many different sources. They can be learned from books, from spiritual advisors, from psychiatrists, or other teachers and Life Coaches. The sources are many. Each of us can choose the one that is the most comfortable and then embrace the wisdom and do the work.

One really excellent tool for maintaining balance is the awareness that all emotions and feelings are really an outgrowth of one of these two emotions: love or fear. Once this concept is embraced it becomes much easier to realize that the fear that is tromping all over your soul is merely fear. In emergency situations, fear tends to take over quickly because of the factor of the unknown. This fear consumes one's soul if you let it.

Fear's original purpose was to move us into fight or flight mode to preserve our life in pre-historic times. The purpose of fear in our modern day culture is more often that of helping us to be aware of potential risk or threats. Once we are aware of this fear, we can circumvent it by our movement into a love based mode. In essence, we creatively dispel its power over us.

> IMPORTANT LEGAL NOTE: At no point will the name of characters, businesses, or associations be used. All such references in this manuscript are to be considered fictional. Again, the author points the reader's attention to the Legal Disclaimer contained within this manuscript. The comments and statements within this manuscript are merely the opinions of the author and are intended to assist Caregivers with suggestions as to how to deal with what may happen and hypothetical situations, and absolutely shall not be considered defamatory or injurious whatsoever.

◦₃

While I was driving to the first hospital to be with John, I had the strangest thoughts pop into my mind. Would John be alright? What has happened to him? Where is his trumpet? Where is our car? I also felt rather numb. I was in shock. It is a good thing I have always been a very good driver. It was difficult to focus on the driving, especially driving someone else's car, during the trip to the hospital where John had been taken. I felt incredibly out of balance and I struggled to maintain control of myself. In rush hour traffic it took me at least an hour to get there.

My next thoughts were of the most profound gratitude: I had requested health insurance for John through my work a mere ninety days prior to this. I believed he would be covered by health insurance. I made an instant decision regarding costs that were not covered by insurance. I would negotiate time payments to medical facilities and doctors. Once I made that decision, some of the panic went away. In retrospect, I am actually amazed I was able to switch into problem solving mode this quickly. I had begun the process of achieving balance for myself in the light of a catastrophic medical emergency.

The first major health insurance issue was that of having the insurance company approve John's treatment in a hospital that was not on our plan. After that moment when the approval came in, I spent my full energy on being present for John and placed the financial issues in the background. This is probably the norm for anyone with emergency health issues. At least I hope it is: people first, money second. The see-saw I was on from "unknown" to "balance" was a regular ride for me during the first several months of this journey.

I truly felt all of this was a moot point anyway and there was no need to worry. In an attempt to find a smidgen of balance among all these unknowns, I just assumed there would be a quick and positive outcome for his health. Naively I believed he would be well soon, and we would work out the details once we knew what was happening.

I will relate only a few examples, in my own opinion, of what occurred for John and me as a result of this insurance. The purpose of relating them is not about putting John and me in victim mode, but to share with you my own personal opinions and lessons we learned from this experience. Since I now know it is no longer in my best interest to harbor negative or judgmental thoughts, I have long since let go of the anger and negative energy of the insurance company events. However, letting go of the negative emotion involved does not mean I have forgotten what occurred. Simply remembering the emotion and the events is completely different than allowing the emotion itself to overtake my days now. It is important that this story be revealed. Hopefully others will benefit from the knowledge of what occurred and learn how to deal with health insurance companies.

CR

There are two major insurance company issues that I believe should never have happened. They also involve smaller issues that occurred within the larger picture of having, in my opinion, a poor quality insurance policy.

The first is when John was moved from one of the finest rehab hospitals in Southern California to the Skilled Nursing Facility or SNF.

Once John was moved, the quality of his therapy and treatment declined severely. He was placed in diapers, which was a real step backward from where he had been at the previous hospital. This was for the convenience of the staff, not because John needed them. His new

Occupational Therapist spent her time with him teaching him to dress himself when he had already achieved this goal. His new Physical Therapist started teaching him a strange method of walking which involved dragging his "weak" leg when John had already begun to learn a normal gait.

I recall being surprised and fearful about all of the backwards steps that occurred upon the move to the SNF! I made several **phone calls** to the insurance company requesting that they change the facility in which they had placed John.

I did not receive a response when I called the insurance company requesting a facility change.

As background information, it was once explained to me how an HMO works. Please note that I will not accept any legal liability for what I relate to the reader in the next paragraph as I am not a health care or legal professional. I am merely giving my personal opinion of what I was once told. I do believe what I was told is a true description of the HMO business model. Nevertheless, the reader must verify and seek professional advice in order to get a fully accurate description of the procedures. I relate here to inform readers of my own personal opinion. That is: find out **how** your insurance works before you buy their product. It may not be the glossy help they sell you when you purchase the insurance. Again, please note the Legal Disclaimer contained within this manuscript.

Summary of how this HMO worked:

There are three layers within the HMO. Layer one at the bottom is the doctor. Layer two in the middle is what is called the "Provider Group". The third layer at the top is the actual insurance company that receives the premium payments from you or your employer. The doctor makes recommendations to the middle company. The middle company makes the decisions about what care will be given and how it will be given. The person in charge of these decisions is a Registered Nurse. Decisions are **not** made by doctors. The top layer company doles out a certain amount of funds for the middle company to spend. These funds are placed in a savings account or a "slush fund" as I call it. The middle level company can only spend whatever amount they have in their "slush fund" for a specific time period. My understanding is that this fund was not patient specific, but it was the total amount they could spend in a given time frame.

In my opinion, here is the real surprise in this scenario: the middle company is sometimes owned by the doctors that belong to the HMO. From a financial standpoint, those owners are probably earning interest on that "slush fund" as long as it is not being spent. Therefore, again in my own personal opinion, it may be to the advantage of their pocket book to delay treatment and any payment for treatment for as long as possible. I feel that they may also deny any treatments that they consider unnecessary if there is a less expensive way.

As I learn more about my insurance company, I feel more and more out of balance and more out of control. I feel enmeshed in a sea of deceit with John treading water in a very stormy sea. All sorts of negative fear-based emotions are roiling among those waves. I feel angry, insignificant, helpless, victimized, and a host of other emotions that have stripped away all my self-esteem. I have been reduced to a fly on the wall, hovering over a sick person that cannot move or speak. The most harmful of these fear-based emotions for me is that I feel powerless. I can do nothing to solve the problems with the insurance company. I am most frightened of all by this last thought.

The Phone Calls continued, and some of these were of a vicious nature.

Soon I started receiving threatening phone calls from collection agencies regarding non-payment for John's treatment and services. These calls were about events that occurred in the hospitals, specific medical treatments, surgery related events, and ambulance rides. The collection agencies told me that the payments for items were over one hundred and twenty days late and thus they had been turned over for "collection" by the service providers. The experience of being in "collection" is not one I would wish on anyone. It involves continual haranguing phone calls and demand letters threatening to damage my credit due to non-payment. This continued for over two years.

I am in shock over the non-payment on the part of the insurance company. Adding to my daily regimen of monitoring John's care and therapy, managing my household, working at the retail store now forty hours a week, teaching twenty five private music students a week, and teaching classes at a music school, it is now necessary for me to make an endless amount of phone calls to the insurance company to find out why the bills are not being paid by them. I guess I get to make these calls from work on my non-existent breaks or from home before or after work.

The scales are tipping further and further away from my finding any sort of balance related to the financial issues of John's care. I feel extremely unbalanced all the time. My stomach is in this continual knot. I cannot sleep at night. This whirlwind of my life every day creates enough negative energy within me to fling anyone into internal rage. It is also no wonder my fatigue is beginning to settle within me at very deep and dark levels. Rage and fatigue and fear. The nightmare roller coaster I am on is endless. This roller coaster is racing up and down from dusk to dawn and back again.

Always floating on the top of my negative sea of emotions, I am in this tiny dinghy of questions on ethics. In what universe is this treatment of family members of patients so inhumane? I thought we paid for insurance to pay for our health care. I cannot wrap my brain around all the infamy regarding payments.

Over the period of about two years while I dealt with these insurance issues, I began to learn a few self-serving tricks that helped me start to come up from the bottom of the non-payment sea. Although I could not force them to make the actual payments, I did learn to find the person responsible for actually making payments.

My arsenal of solutions follows.

Solutions for Dealing with the Insurance Issues

Get a notebook and write down dates and times of every call you receive and make.

Record phone numbers and extension numbers on every call.

Write down the name of the person to whom you spoke and paraphrase what they told you. Get their "job title" and write that down.

Read your insurance policy and make sure you understand what they agreed to pay for, and what your financial responsibilities are.

From my own personal experiences and in my opinion, be prepared to be misdirected, placed on hold, disconnected, and to be subjected to large amounts of prevarication.

Keep all of your bills together and as organized as possible. You will be deluged with paper. The amount of paper is an indication, to me, of one of the reasons why insurance costs so much.

As challenging as this concept is, this insurance game is not about YOU. Do not take it personally. To the insurance company, it is simply business.

Please do not get involved emotionally in the methodology of any insurance company. Their business model is beyond your control. Stay positive in your outlook and simply go through the motions, not the emotions of what you need to do. Remember that your health and the health of your loved one are the most important.

LESSONS LEARNED

I discovered that certain bills were paid by the top level insurance company and some were scheduled to be paid by the middle level group. The method they used to determine who paid what, in my mind, is their hidden business model. I spent a lot of time just trying to get to the right person at the right company to try and determine what was paid or not paid.

> I learned that using the "titles" of those who were actually in charge of the payments was a faster way to get through the phone bank system to the right person. I spoke to supervisors whenever possible. It is my belief, that most likely only the supervisors were the ones who had the true information of what payments were paid.
>
> I finally realized what I believed their game was: create as much obfuscation as possible, and withhold payments for as long as possible. If they did not make the payments in a timely fashion, it did not hurt the credit of their company. The vendors would simply send it out for "collection" and the patient's family would take the hit on their credit. I felt, that as long as the insurance company did not make the payments, the money was in their slush fund earning interest for the doctors. This is only my opinion based upon my own personal experience.

✺

The second major insurance issue was the most frightening for me. It occurred when John had the surgery to correct his congenitally defective carotid artery. I must say that both John and I are extremely grateful that the insurance company agreed to allow John to have this corrective surgery. It has saved his life. However, the process of the actual surgery was another matter.

This surgery occurred about a year after the stroke. John was admitted to the hospital and his surgery occurred in the morning. I was directed to a small family waiting room next to the Intensive Care Unit. My understanding was that after the surgery, John would be moved to a Recovery Room, and once he was fully awake, he would be moved to Intensive Care where he would be monitored and cared for by the best of the staff until he was stable. While I was waiting in that small room, the doors suddenly opened and John was wheeled through this family waiting room on a gurney into the Intensive Care Unit. I asked the attendant if I could follow along. They cheerfully gave me permission to come with them.

The next event was totally shocking to me. I felt that the nurse at the nurses' station was screaming at me! Her screams were, "Who are you? What are you doing in here? You cannot be in here!!! Get out of here right now." Since I had just been told I could come in there, I related that information to the nurse. She would have nothing of this and continued screaming at me. Wow. I had never been treated in such a manner before in my life.

I decided that I would retrace my steps and I went back to the family waiting room. I am sure there are many more acceptable ways of asking me to leave, but screaming at the top of her lungs would not have been my first choice for behavior on the part of a professional. It left a lot of doubt in my mind as to the skills of those who were caring for John. This unprofessional treatment of me was really just a sideline event relative to the major event that followed the next day.

An hour or so later, another nurse came out and retrieved me so I could see John. It was late afternoon by now and I was only allowed a short time to visit with him. I went home for the night.

One would think there would have been some sort of plan for his care and that John's family would be notified of this plan. No one prepared me for the event that was to occur the next morning.

I arrived at the hospital early the next morning to visit with John a bit before I had to go to work. He was still in Intensive Care. While I was in the room a nurse walked in and told me that John would be going home before noon. Or, he would leave as soon as his vital statistics returned to normal; whichever came first. I totally freaked! I called work and told them I could not come in today as I had to bring John home from the hospital and care for him. I had about two hours of warning to prepare for taking care of someone who was still in Intensive Care. I called my friend, the nurse, and asked her what to do. She told me that surgery patients are normally downgraded to a regular hospital room signifying their stability and readiness to leave the hospital. It makes the hospital's liability much less.

This was frightening event number two. I believe the insurance company was counting dollars and they did not want to pay for the downgrade room to monitor John. I also felt they were counting the number of hours in the Intensive Care room and did not want to pay for another day of Intensive Care, either. Let me stress here: I believe this decision was not made by the hospital or by John's surgeon. Rather, I believe it was the insurance company that made the decision. John had just had major surgery twenty-four hours prior, and his "normal vitals" status had lasted only sixty seconds when he was sent home from his hospital bed in Intensive Care. I went out, pulled the car around to the door, loaded John from the hospital wheelchair into our car and took him home.

At this point in John's physical recovery from the stroke he was able to walk up the stairs into our home with assistance. I had his wheelchair waiting inside the door. I moved him to the couch in the living room and made him comfortable. His speech ability was extremely minimal at this point. He could not tell me what was wrong, if something was wrong, or how he felt.

From my point of view, it was like caring for an infant in that the Caregiver can only guess and then react based upon the best information that they have at that moment.

Fortunately, my friend the rehab nurse lived close by. She came over and taught me how to take care of someone who was just released from Intensive Care. Among other things, she told me the most important thing was to check his temperature because that was an indication of infection. She told me to call her anytime if I suspected anything was wrong.

I made a desperate attempt to appear balanced during this event for John's sake. Most certainly I did not feel balanced. I felt panicked and overwhelmed. I was on the downhill ride of the extreme roller coaster in the medical theme park.

On the positive side of this event, I am so grateful that my friend was a nurse and was available to help me learn what to do in this circumstance. Angels were certainly watching over both John and me and giving me the presence of mind to manage his care. I was learning that it is far better to remain positive and in control of one's emotions than to succumb to fear.

Solutions for the Caregiver

Keep your wits about you and follow the instructions carefully on any release paperwork given to you by the medical facilities.

If you know someone in the health care industry, remain friends with them and ask them for assistance. If they are truly your friend they will share ideas or hints on what to do. They cannot be held liable, of course, but they can tell you what to watch for as far as symptoms are concerned.

This may sound silly or extremely obvious, but have your home well stocked with basic medical supplies. This includes bandages, a thermometer, sterile water for bathing wounds, and lots of clean sheets and towels. Wow, can you go through towels and sheets quickly!

Improvise and be flexible. Your ability to bend with the wind of whatever the Universe or the insurance company sends your way will serve you much better than allowing fear to overwhelm you.

LESSONS LEARNED

No one knows the future. All we have is "the now". Relax and rejoice in your strength at this moment.

See the fourth paragraph in the box above. It is both a solution and a lesson.

Focus on keeping your emotions in the "love" arena, not the "fear" arena. Love serves you and allows you to think clearly. Fear does not serve you and can take your brain away from being able to think at all. If you cannot think, you cannot find solutions. Staying with love-based emotions is truly the only way to remain balanced.

It is my opinion that everyone should pay for quality health insurance above all else. I felt that dealing with this company was a total nightmare for the first three years after John's stroke. This is the nightmare that kept me out of balance for a long time. I vowed many times that I would never be involved in an HMO again. In my opinion, this insurance company was not about providing what John needed. I felt that its goal was to see how little they could actually do for him and I believe their entire purpose was to provide the bare minimum of what their policy with us required. I felt that their methodology was money first, people second. Again, to be clear, this is only my opinion and I direct the reader's attention to the Legal Disclaimer contained within this manuscript.

○○

Three years after the stroke, at the point when the term "pre-existing condition" usually becomes a moot point in qualifying for insurance benefits, I could now move away from my job at the retail store. In order to change our personal financial situation, it was imperative that I find better paying work. Since John's pre-existing condition was no longer an issue, I could purchase different health insurance for him.

After several stints with a temporary agency, the Universe rewarded me with a job at a local university in the music library. This opportunity provided two main things: it tripled my monthly income and it provided quality health insurance for both of us. We both now had a PPO, or Preferred Provider Organization plan. This meant that we had access to specialists as long as they were in our network. John could finally see a neurologist and have his seizure disorder managed by extremely competent physicians. When we used the new insurance, the bills were paid and I never received another call from a collection agency. Medications were provided and a certain amount of therapy each year was covered by the insurance. Balance was returning to our lives.

CR

LESSONS LEARNED

The most important lesson I learned during this series of events was this: always have quality health insurance that is PPO based. In a PPO, one's doctor makes the decisions about what care is given. If one wishes to see a specialist, all one needs to do is ask. One's doctor can request them or one can make the appointments. One's personal control over what happens and the quality of the service provided is far superior in a PPO. It is worth whatever money one needs to pay to move up this ladder.

Being in control of the decision making process and choosing doctors that are in one's preferred provider network helps achieve balance as a Caregiver. This

> balance is essential to one's wellbeing. If one feels balanced and has a sense of control over the situation, then one will be able to be a better Caregiver. Decisions are easier to make. One will make better decisions because of having a clear mind. One's sense of purpose can be to provide the best possible solutions for one's loved one and for one's self. Maintain as much balance as possible.

Additional suggestions for keeping in balance are the following:

- Meditate: it calms the mind.
- Maintain your spiritual practice: it nourishes the soul.
- Keep your emotional state in the love-based realm, not the fear-based realm: it helps create clarity and balance.

CR

Now that I had the care and treatment of both of our health in the realm of being treated like human beings, I was able to move into more love-based emotions myself. This allowed me to realize it was those negative events that moved me into the path of learning to find the solutions we needed. As I found more and more solutions, I gained confidence in my ability to handle any situation with grace and ease. Most importantly, I realized the strength and balance that I had gained as a result of this journey resulted in the creation of space in my soul. This is the space for peace.

Years later, as I review this process, I know that this was the path that we were given to follow because of the spiritual growth that resulted for us. The result of our learning, growth and change, is what has brought great joy and peace to both of us.

Spaciousness

*How do we stay balanced
on the ever-turning wheel of change?
By moving to the center
and letting the wheel spin as it will.
By remaining empty,
making room for all the feelings that arise
in ourselves and others.*

*The myriad events of whirling life
are the materials of our work.
The spaciousness within
is where the work is done.*

"The Caregiver's Tao Te Ching" by William and Nancy Martin

Chapter 4

Happy Accidents are Miracles and Gifts

A Happy Accident is defined by potters as an unexpected result that is particularly beautiful. It occurs when a function of the clay handling process by a potter or the firing process in a kiln results in a surprise. Other terms that are similar to the Happy Accident concept are serendipity, gifts, and miracles. I am grateful that language has provided several positive energy words for the many wonderful things that happen in our daily lives.

Many such things have happened to John and me in the years since his stroke. They are especially wonderful because we learned so many lessons while we reviewed the events that were part of the process of life unfolding for us. Most importantly, we learned to look for the Happy Accidents! The realization that something miraculous occurred while we were doing something else has been a source of much joy for both of us.

Nancy Weckwerth

☙

During a recent move from one city to another after we sold our first house, I lost my car keys for my Mustang. They disappeared in our new apartment on a Tuesday (or was it a Wednesday?) during the first (or was it the second?) week of January. I did not write down the day. Gratefully, I have two vehicles and even more gratefully, the car was parked in the apartment lot, not in the street when this occurred. This was my only key and it was one of those smart keys that cost up to $300 to replace at a dealership. I did not have the money to replace the key, so until I did, I decided to drive the old Mazda truck. It runs great and gets better mileage than the Mustang anyway. I do not have to tell you which vehicle is more fun and comfortable to drive.

It is now April. Like the two meandering melodies in a Bach fugue, two weeks ago I had an unexpected check arrive in the mail. Plus, I found my emergency stash of cash in a box I unpacked. Between the two minor miracles, I had enough money for the new key. I called a locksmith and two hours later had a shiny brand new key for the discount price of $185. The third miracle: it was less than $300!

Synchronicity is an amazing thing. A few days later, while I was explaining to John what a "Happy Accident "was, I reached up on a bookshelf to show him my first ever raku fired piece of pottery. As stated earlier, potters consider unexpected glaze outcomes of fired pots "Happy

Accidents" from the Japanese traditional potters' lore. At least that was the lore in the pottery studio in which I used to work. Thus any raku pottery can be considered a Happy Accident. The result is always unknown, and most of the time, beautiful. I picked up my rookie handmade raku pot from the bookshelf and discovered my car keys had fallen into the pot. Here is the synchronicity: the Happy Accident of finding my keys, was inside the Happy Accident of a beautiful raku pot, while I was explaining what a Happy Accident was. It was a magical moment and resulted in a stunned silence from me.

I decided "Happy Accident" is the absolute perfect title for this chapter.

ɞ

Since the tragedy of John's stroke has long since disappeared for us, we daily view it as the gift of a Happy Accident. Please do not be stunned by this honest revelation.

The positive lessons that have been given to both John and I as a result of his CVA are incredible and multitudinous. I will share many of these gifts in this chapter. The gifts are a result of the Happy Accident concept. It is really about sharing a lot of lemonade that has been made and enjoyed between the two of us through the past twenty-five years. I hope that you will be able to discover the Happy Accidents in your life as you meet the challenges of living with a person with brain damage or a handicap. Like a finely crafted Mozart piano sonata, each Happy Accident has become a part of the mellifluous melody of our journey.

༄

On trusting your own judgment

One of the gifts we have been given is the knowledge that if your gut tells you the medical personnel with whom you are working are not serving your best interests, change medical personnel. Trust yourself first.

John developed a seizure disorder so he was placed on anticonvulsant medication. I believe I was told that: "Stroke patients have a period of time during the healing process from nine months to about two and a half years when the brain is healing. It is called the Seizure Window. Frequently the growing scar tissue in the brain bumps a nerve and sets off a seizure. John will be medicated with the smallest amount of anticonvulsant possible and gradually add more until he stops having seizures. This will be the amount of drug needed by him and will interfere less with his brain function." I felt unsure of this process. In retrospect, I wish I would have followed my own intuition as I later learned that what I was told may have been inaccurate.

John had a total of seventeen grand mal seizures during the seizure window. I would rush him to the hospital ER in the middle of the night and have his blood tested for anticonvulsant levels. I was beside myself from carrying a catatonic one-hundred-sixty-pound man out of the house, loading him into the car, changing soiled bed linens, and other things that occur with seizures. We kept upping the dosage of his medication. I was even told at some point, that John did not have enough medication in his body to stop an infant from having seizures.

Although I made every effort to get John to see a neurologist, I did not have the financial resources available to do it privately. It is my understanding that neurologists are the physicians of choice for anyone with brain damage and seizure disorders.

When we went to the next appointment, John's normal PCP was on vacation and we got a "substitute" doctor. Talk about a Happy Accident! I told him about John's history of seizures and what I was told about treatment. The Doctor-Sub left the room and returned with a Physician's Desk Reference. He showed me the recommended treatment for stroke patient seizures which was what I believe was exactly the opposite of what I was initially told. The medically-recommended method is to start them at the highest recommended dosage for their age and weight and gradually lower the dosage until they have a seizure. This would mean John would have had two seizures instead of seventeen.

Looking back on this now, I did not listen to my gut enough on this series of events. I felt something was wrong with the treatment but did not take strong action to save both John and me a lot of fear and pain. The eventual gift arrived about this series of events when I learned that we were given this as a means of learning an important lesson and I repeat: if your gut does not trust the current medical personnel, change medical personnel. I cannot stress this enough. We have all heard the "get a second opinion" concept. It is absolutely true. If the first concerto is disharmonious, get more manuscript paper off the shelf and start re-composing the music around you.

Seek out the gifts and Happy Accidents of "lessons learned" in your situation and be grateful for them. Breathe, deeply. Take the time to analyze what is happening instead of only reacting to it. Look for the bigger picture. The analysis will help you see the gifts. Sometimes the gifts are transparent and immediately obvious. Sometimes they appear in another movement in the symphony of life. It is about the attitude of "always seeking gifts" as they are positive thoughts. Positive thoughts attract more positive things to you.

The best gift for having done this will be joy and peace for you, and for your loved one.

☙

On learning new skills

Self-reliance or taking responsibility for your loved one's therapy on your own may become necessary as health insurance benefits wane, or as your finances dwindle.

It also encompasses more than just the Caregiver. It is about teamwork. This teamwork attitude is one of the greatest gifts John and I developed as an outcome of the loving relationship we had. We both learned many new skills along this path of recovery for him.

As mentioned previously, John and I made a pact to become partners in the solution finding for successful outcomes for his CVA. Our life became one long therapy session. We were able to do therapy almost constantly because it was usually gift wrapped in laughter and fun.

Because our attitude was that of choice and gratitude, John and I worked on therapy at home by ourselves almost every waking moment. We stopped when we slept or when other tasks were the priority of the moment. I read books on speech therapy, listened and watched John's Occupational Therapist (OT) and Physical Therapist (PT) and helped John practice all of those whenever we could. Since both of us had been professional musicians, we were gratefully addicted to practice and repetition. Since both of us also had past careers in education, we knew the path of starting with basic skills and building upon them.

I became an active observer in all the therapy sessions with the professionals. All the while that John was learning "new" skills like balance, walking, and re-building muscles, I was learning how this can be accomplished. Because we were both learning the "how" of this process, his therapy did not stop when he left the therapist's gym or when the therapist left our home. In addition to learning from them, I found books in the library on speech therapy. I also found textbooks on the Internet that we purchased and used.

One Happy Accident in this aspect of John's recovery was that I discovered the children's bookstore section of many different stores. I practiced the new skill of seeking out our own solutions. Since John's mind was in many ways a clear slate, like a child's, we used children's books on learning to read, learning math, and so forth. The children's bookstore sections have a plethora of kindergarten, 1st, 2nd, and 3rd grade reading workbooks. These are basic skill building workbooks that are easily accessible for anyone to buy. They are inexpensive.

Lunch became assignment time. For example, one assignment was to do one page of recognizing all the "a" letters on a page by circling them. We did not always use the books the way they were intended. However, after a few months, John would take these out on his own, without my initiation, and work on them. He enjoyed the process of learning the skills again. He knew it was helping him. He did not know the "why" of what was happening in that these tasks were reconfiguring his brain and creating new neural pathways. He experienced great joy by having success at what he was doing. For him it was a magical rediscovery of language.

Some professional therapists may take umbrage with this method because they stress always "treating the patient like an adult" not like a child. In our case, I knew John's personality and his level of intelligence. John is a highly intelligent man with a Master's Degree from Yale and a DMA (Doctor of Musical Arts) from the University of Miami in music composition. We discussed the concept of using those materials for the skill-building they offered, not because he was a child using children's materials. Just because they had lots of simple drawings, sometimes bright colors, and simple tasks, does not mean they were inappropriate for an adult. John understood this because of his background in teaching. Actually, because of their simple level, we could focus on one basic skill at a time and very gradually rebuild the skills he needed to speak again.

Successful use of these materials was about our attitude towards what we were doing. I never commented about the age appropriateness of the materials. I truly believe that the simplicity of the materials we used eliminated the distractions of more complex learning tools. Learning to add a correct verb into a sentence from a list of verbs is the same skill whether you are a child or an adult. I know these types of daily exercises on our part contributed to the success of John's return to the land of "speaking". In actuality, the simplicity of the skills, one very basic skill at a time, accompanied by drawings that were context appropriate helped him immensely. His brain power was stretched to the max to do these simple things.

Sometimes the skill was too hard. Then I would change the assignment on the page. For example, we often used pre-school music lesson books to teach him the skills of reading and writing music again. If there was a picture of a keyboard on the page and they were to color all the "A" keys red, he could not read and follow the written instructions simultaneously. John could read but not speak. This is a brain damage "thing" where he could read the instructions, but the bridge between reading the instructions and **doing** what the instructions said was broken. He also has extreme difficulty in using full sentences. Most of his speech is in short phrases that he cannot connect into a sentence. The technical term for this condition is Broca's Aphasia. In order to create a bridge for him, without saying anything, I would take a red crayon or marker and color the first "A" on the keyboard red. He immediately understood what his assignment was. I would leave and come back to check on his work. He initiated his own methodology. I would come back to all the As red, Bs blue, Cs yellow and so forth. He actually created his own learning opportunity. This shows how strong his desire was to come back from the gray corner his life had become.

I have admired his courage from the first day of his stroke. He was and is an amazing student. He wanted to learn and come back to the world. He still cannot follow written instructions. That skill has never returned. Our Happy Accident discovery of appropriate materials for him made the difference for his transition back to the world of the "speaking".

◊

On building upon old skills

I am eternally grateful, as is John, that we had been teachers. It was an incredible gift that our previous skills suited our present needs. Our attitude of "all opportunities are for learning" helped us find ways to work together to give John the gift of speech again.

John's speech is not perfect. He is expressive aphasic. He has many moments of "difficult to communicate" to quote him. Over the years he continually surprises me with vocabulary additions that have come out of nowhere. John often speaks in sentences but he still has many moments of frustration. However, his vocabulary and speech ability is way beyond the one hundred and fifty words we were initially told was his limit. We chose not to be limited. This has been the greatest gift we have given ourselves.

Interestingly enough, John's ability to converse in the subject of music is by far his best conversational topic. He can discuss musical compositions, compositional techniques, and composers with ease. His knowledge of what piece is being performed on the classical cable television station is phenomenal. He can still name the composer of every piece. He knows the life history of most of the great composers. A few years ago we attended an opera performance of Richard Wagner's "Der Ring des Nibelungen" or "Ring Cycle" with a friend. John knew and was able to explain to a limited degree the story of each of the operas to us. He is truly amazing.

ଔ

Another Happy Accident that resulted because of lessons learned throughout this entire adventure has been that we know that everyone has to follow their own path. Everything stated in this book is intended to help others discover that they can choose to find their own solutions. Our solutions may not work for others. It is about finding one's own solutions to their unique situational challenges. If we found solutions, so can everyone. Be at peace and know that the solutions are there! We now live in joy because we found so many solutions. Laughter fills our lives. We share the wisdom of having success to the highest degree possible for John because of our choices and solutions.

ଔ

On therapy

Gratefully, one doctor said to me in the early days of our journey: "Remember, John will always improve."

We knew that the best natural healing and recovery period was immediately after the onset of the stroke. The first month is optimum, the next three months are the first benchmark, and medical re-evaluation occurs at the six month period. Another practitioner said that after two years, most of his natural healing and improvement would have been achieved.

Some "unexpected events" that have a positive result could also be called serendipitous. They are also Happy Accidents, as defined on the Internet, in that they are a combination of an unexpected, not necessarily misfortunate event with a positive result. Serendipity is the term I will use to describe miraculously unexpected events that have positive results.

There were many shining stars that serendipitously appeared in our lives just as we needed them. I totally believe the Universe provides what you need when you need it, if you just observe that phenomenon.

The brightest of these stars is an Occupational Therapist, often abbreviated as OT named "Kaley". Three days after John's stroke, she walked into the retail store where I was working and was speaking to my boss. My boss brought me over and said "I think you should meet this woman." This was the most serendipitous event of all. She specializes in treating musicians with hand injuries.

We arranged for private therapy with Kaley. Her wisdom, skill, and professional network connections in the greater Los Angeles area, placed us within a circle of top therapists and a variety of types of therapy. Kaley provided timely referrals to other therapists. Since this was a private venture, she was not limited to recommending the therapists in any specific clinic, hospital, or health insurance group. She set us up with the best therapists for John during the various stages in his recovery. We are very grateful for her skills on many levels.

Kaley went into the Skilled Nursing Facility two nights a week and worked as a private therapist for us. She used her Neurodevelopmental Training, also known as NDT, to establish neural-muscular education facilitating the development of a new foundation while reactivating any former pathways in the following areas:

- Sitting, Static and Dynamic Balance
- Weight Bearing
- Weight Shifting

John had lost all of those skills as a result of his stroke.

Initially in John's recovery, the goal was to get him to a 25%-75% ratio where he participated with 25% of the movement and/or control to help the therapists or nurses do 75% of the Activities of Daily Living, or ADLs. This 25%-75% ratio is called maximum assistance. Static balance refers to the ability to initiate and regain balance when sitting or standing still. Dynamic balance refers to the ability to initiate and regain balance when in motion. One of John's first accomplishments was to be able to sit up while being dressed or while eating. John's participation with even this small amount of movement and physical control as early as possible was critical.

This early control was an indication of the likelihood of eventual independence in his ADLs.

By the fourth week in his recovery John had learned to stand, or do weight bearing, on his legs while dressing, transferring to a wheelchair, or in the bathroom. He also relearned weight shifting. Weight shifting assisted his Caregivers while dressing in that John had to be able to shift his weight from one leg to the other while putting on each pant leg. These were significant gains that met rehabilitation criteria to continue treatment.

Goals were continually moved up for John, and when the new goals were met and documented in his records, it was a means of tracking his improvement. In theory, the insurance company would pay for his care as long as John showed improvement.

Kaley continued to work with John regularly for the first three years and on an "as needed" for the first ten years. More than anything, Kaley's smile and positive attitude would melt a mountain of ice in the blinking of an eye. Twenty-five years later, we are still close friends with Kaley.

This was and is serendipity at its finest.

ꙮ

On creating quality of life

One of the things that fit into the plan of creating quality for John, was for us to buy our own home. The rental house where we lived when the stroke occurred, by its very nature of being a rental, meant that the accommodations John needed to have more quality of life at home were not changes I could make. John needed to be able to bathe on his own, go for walks on a sidewalk in a safe neighborhood, and be able to practice his trumpet. He will tell you that the importance of the items in the last sentence is in the reverse order that I just stated them.

I spoke to family members and they were able to provide some of the down-payment money for us. This money was on a loan basis and was to be re-paid as interest-only monthly payments. At some point in the future, the money was inevitably to be John's inheritance. In reality, the down-payment was an investment in California property for family members. Their return on investment was interest payments from us.

After several months of shopping for homes in our price range, the Universe provided a perfect home for us. In addition to the normal bedrooms, bath, living room, dining room and kitchen, the home had two rooms and a bath that had been added on by the previous owner with the sound proofing for a recording studio. John could practice his trumpet to his heart's content in his studio and he was steps away from his private bath. The other added room, was a studio for me where I could teach my private students in a separate area, away from the living room where John watched television. Talk about a Happy Accident!

There was a sidewalk out front and the neighborhood was perfect. In addition, there was even a private alley in the back that provided safety where John could go for a walk daily. He walked out the door of his studio, through the yard to the alley, to the corner, then around to the front door of the house on the sidewalk. The total distance of this walk was maybe sixty yards. It took him forty-five minutes to accomplish this. Most of us walk this in two-three minutes. He did this walk several times a week for about twelve to fifteen years.

☙

These are only a few of the Happy Accidents in our lives. I often describe our lives as "making a lot of lemonade." Through the happenstance of our wake-up call, John and I live much better now than we could have imagined. It is different than we planned, but better. You may ask that since we did not ever reach our initial career goal of being high level professional musicians in Los Angeles for many years, how do we know that this life is better than that life would have been, had we been allowed to fulfill that goal? Life is a crap-shoot. We do not know what will occur. All we can do is move through it with the best possible attitude, change as needed via analysis and taking action, and living in gratitude for the lessons learned.

Above all, John and I have learned gratitude. This is the greatest gift. All along our journey, the Universe has supported us by giving us what we needed, when we needed it. Most of these gifts were and still are, **lessons**.

From deep inside my soul, I feel that the peace, laughter, and gratitude that fills our lives daily is much better than the high level pressure of performing at the top of the heap for us. We still have contact with many of our pre-stroke musician friends, and the litany of their lives is no longer something we desire. Our awareness of the Happy Accidents of our journey through this life has given us a different joy. As we learned these lessons, and stopped grasping for our past life of professional music performance, we found this different joy and ultimately much more peace. Who is to say which joy or peace is best? We have certainly chosen to be full of joy. The peace simply arrived in the symphony of our life with each miracle, with each gift, and with the discovery of each Happy Accident.

It Happened by Itself

*All our striving seems to push away
the very peace we are seeking.
We grasp for hope,
and it eludes us.
We stretch for safety,
and it remains evasive.*

*When we cease striving
and stop grasping and stretching,
we find that we are carried by the Tao.
What we tried to accomplish by our efforts
we find has happened by itself.*

"The Caregiver's Tao Te Ching" by William and Nancy Martin

Chapter 5

The Caregiver's Health

> The most important rule for all of us,
> but especially for Caregivers:
>
> **Take care of yourself first, so that
> you can take care of others.**

Learning this rule was one of my biggest challenges as a Caregiver. I still struggle with it daily as it does not come naturally for me to take care of myself. The life I had always lived was one of building. I firmly believe that success is a result of building upon and developing one's natural talents. My focus has always been the "career", and the build of that career. The career was the goal, the impetus of every thought in my head. Taking care of my "self" rarely entered my train of thought throughout the day until I had been a Caregiver for several years. I truly think that I had to make the shift to thinking of myself as a Caregiver on a long term basis before I was able to let go of the "career-thought methodology."

Don't Stop the Music

The intention of the following anecdote is to paint a picture of our lifestyle before the stroke. It explains the intensity of each day: the eternal drive to become a success as professional musicians for both of us. The story of our daily lives explains the reason why I had to learn the ultimate lesson: to take care of myself first, after I became a Caregiver. It shows my growth and learning as I went through the change from musician to Caregiver with love and joy.

ɶ

Prior to February 12, 1991, the first day of John's stroke, our lives as professional musicians were a whirlwind of practicing, writing music, performing, marketing ourselves for additional work, practicing, rehearsing, writing the music for the next performance or "gig" as musicians call them, publishing the music in our publishing company, and of course, performing, rehearsing and practicing. What joy!

Daily chores such as eating, cooking, cleaning, laundry, shopping for groceries, and taking care of the crucial automobile that got us to and from gigs were a "major second" in our lives. Then there is the small ordeal of paying bills and taxes. We lived by our schedule calendar and the answering machine on our phone. This was before cell phones with voice mail. All these items were mere details in our busy and exciting lives. Our business was growing. Our skills as artists were expanding. Our reputations were getting stronger in the music world of Los Angeles. We were so grateful!

When our phone rang, it was about work and this was about getting paid. We scheduled ourselves silly. Every gig was an opportunity to be "in the right place" and to be with "the right people" to get hired for the next gig. Every free rehearsal was another marketing opportunity for us. We created and mailed brochures, made demo tapes, and mailed out more demo tapes.

The next gig was always around the corner.

The danger is this: you can never turn down a job, or they will not call you again. Availability is everything. Making friends on the job was more than everything: it is the way that you build your reputation. It has been said that once you reach a certain skill level on your performing instrument, it is more about how you get along with the others on the gig. It truly becomes "who you know" and whether or not you get along with them. It has to be fun for everyone.

Both of us worked the typical free-lance symphony, opera, and the occasional recording session. We played with brass quintets, brass quartets, brass trios, and booked any of these and all of these whenever we could. To accommodate the type of music that was required on these jobs, John and I both wrote and arranged the necessary music for the gig. If the music was original or the arrangements were in the public domain, meaning

Don't Stop the Music

the copyright had expired, we published the music in our growing publishing company, Trombacor Music.

For years prior to John's stroke, we lived in Toronto, Canada. Our main reason to move from Toronto to Los Angeles was to find the skill set and level of musicians required to perform in John's dream group, Rising Winds. John created the concept of this ten piece wind ensemble that had 1 trumpet, 1 (French)[1] horn, 1 trombone, 1 tuba, 1 flute, 1 clarinet, 1 oboe, 1 bassoon, 1 percussionist, and 1 bass player. The concept extended to include the fact that everyone had to be both a classical player and be able to improvise jazz. All of the woodwind players doubled on all of the other woodwind instruments, too. That meant that the flute player also played alto and bass flute, and clarinet. The clarinet player played flute, and all the saxophones. The oboe player played clarinet, flute, and all saxophones. The bassoon player played all saxophones and clarinet. The percussionist had a veritable army of percussion instruments and timpani. The bass player usually played upright bass. This wide variety of instrumentation provided for a lot of color. The addition of jazz to each person's skill set created an ensemble that was new on the face of the earth.

---

[1] Note: The name of this instrument was officially changed to Horn by the International Horn Society in the 1960s. In America, many still call it the French Horn. Most countries in the world call it the "horn". In this book, hereafter it will be called "horn".

This group was John's passion. He wrote new pieces incessantly. We booked the group as often as possible in concert venues. We created brochures, made demo tapes, and marketed this ensemble with all of our energy. Rehearsals were at the music union rehearsal halls every Friday morning at 10:30. I wrote and arranged a few works for the group but the bulk of the compositions were John's. A few of the other composer members also wrote works. One of those compositions by other members was actually entitled "Friday Morning at 10:30."

The other musicians in the group loved the music, the level of performance, the style, and of course John's sense of humor. It was an opportunity for everyone to show off all of their skills at very high levels in one ensemble. It was musicians' music. Although the real quality of what happened with that group probably went over the heads of most audiences, they always applauded. It did not matter what the audiences thought about the music to John. It did not really matter to any of the other performers either. It was a chance to really play and extend ourselves. As difficult as it is to admit, most gigs musicians have are routine and the real issue is boredom. Most gigs are about pleasing the audience—letting them hear what they recognize so they will buy another ticket. Rising Winds was at the other end of the spectrum. It was true art for art's sake. Marketable? Who cared.

CR

Because of our lifestyle, when the stroke happened, my immediate reaction was: Don't Stop the Music!

For over a year after the stroke, I was determined to continue with John's dream for Rising Winds and other musical endeavors. Naively, for all I knew, he would be back performing and writing soon. I practiced my instruments, wrote music, completed the paperwork for the IRS 501 c3 non-profit status of Rising Winds, booked concerts as I could, and conducted the group in John's absence. Of course this was on top of taking care of John, the full time job at the retail store, teaching about twenty to twenty-five private students a week, and organizing John's twelve to fifteen therapy appointments a week.

When John was in one hospital, one social worker once said to me, "Who is going to do the shopping?" I looked at her like she was an alien from another planet. Shopping was no big deal. I usually did it on the way home from a concert at midnight in my "concert blacks" (a term used by musicians to describe the black tuxedos or other black clothing on stage). At that point, shopping being an issue was not even on my radar. Re-creating John's life and following our dream was all that was important.

ʘ

Soon my awareness became that if I went down, everything went down. This developed into a new reflection in my daily mental activity. The reflection grew to become a constant shadow lingering in the self-preservation instinct of my soul. Like the sounding board in a piano, I had to be strong enough to support the pressure of all of the many strings that produce the sound–the music in our lives.

Because I was growing to understand my new position as Caregiver on the team, I realized that I needed to make sure my health was up to the stressful tasks to come. I knew I could not take care of him if I was ill, too. The first thing I did to monitor my health occurred about a month after the stroke. I went to my doctor and had my vitals checked to make sure my stress level was neither causing health issues for me, nor causing my blood pressure to rise. I learned I was healthy on all counts so moved forward with the task of taking care of everything that needed to be taken care of to bring John back to his former self.

ೕ

I became almost fanatical about time management. In order to keep up this pace, I realized it was critical to make the most out of every hour of the day as there was no time to waste. Each day became honed for absolute efficiency. In order to function, I had to develop a plan for ultimate efficiency in everything that I did. This extreme efficiency allowed me to achieve as much as was humanly possible in the least amount of time. It meant always multitasking.

> **Solutions for Time Management:**
>
> I did laundry while I was teaching my private students at home and while another therapist was working with John in the dining room. I did not have a dryer, only a washer, so I often did laundry before work, hung clothes on the line early in the morning and took them off the line when I came home from the retail store.
>
> I prepared a lot of crock pot meals for John and I that cooked while we were sleeping and fed us good healthy food for days.
>
> I bought a portable dishwasher in week three of the journey. I did not have the time to do dishes.
>
> I quickly maximized our computer's ability to pay bills online. I also automated as many of our bills as possible. They paid themselves as long as I kept depositing the funds for them to do so. Every bill paid this way was a task that was "off" my brain.

Another example of the solution finding was at my job in the retail store. Although it was only a few blocks from the house where we lived, it became much more efficient and effective for me to take John to work with me. My bosses graciously allowed this. I could make sure he was OK without having to run home and check on him throughout the day. This solution was much more efficient for everyone. Problem solved.

The local library was a short distance away from my job. I would take John in his wheelchair to the library for hours. Sometimes he rolled himself back to the retail store. All the librarians knew him, and he carried my phone number with him. He read incessantly. What a blessing this was on so many counts. He was re-developing his brain skills, entertaining himself, and was in a safe place. There were caring people around if there was a need for help.

Taking care of the family pets became another issue for me to solve time-wise. Our blessed cats ate dry food from a large bulk feeder for two years and did not complain about the lack of variety. Any of you who have ever had cats know that this is a miracle in itself. They sensed that I was maxed-out and their version of helping was to eat whatever was available. They were amazing friends providing companionship and compassion throughout the journey for both of us.

As time passed in this frenzy of my activity, one thing I discovered was that all of us have an internal reserve of energy that we can call upon in stressful times. At first I ran on adrenalin because of the enormous demands placed upon me at my job, the need to take care of the house, take care of the finances, do all laundry, dishes, housecleaning, taking care of John and doing therapy with him daily. The organizational and time management skills I developed during this time helped me conserve my ever dwindling source of internal reserve energy.

At about two and a half years into John's recovery, I realized that I was burning my internal reserve without replenishing it. One of the symptoms of this was that I developed a severe sleeping disorder. I could not sleep. My brain was racing through all of the organizational items for the next day, and the next, and the next.

I also could not sleep in our bed. I just moved to the couch permanently. It gave me some peace from dealing with John's paralysis all night long, especially when he started having seizures. It gave me a little "space" for myself. The toll on my health was only starting to become apparent.

I was beginning to actually experience severe fatigue both from the frenzy of my pace and the lack of sleep. I felt I was starting to fall down. I was coming apart at the seams physically. I feared the entire structure of the music, John's recovery, and our world would fail. Failure was not an option.

CR

In spite of all of the efficiency and solution finding, it was at the two and a half year point in this marathon that I realized that something had to stop for me. I could not possibly do it all anymore. I felt my energy and my stamina had disappeared into a black abyss of nothingness. I had reached a point of no return. I had nowhere to reach inside of myself anymore to pull out another day, another decision, another phone call to a doctor or to the insurance company.

I pondered daily on what else I had to do to stop my energy drain in order to preserve my health. Initially, my thought process was to remove additional unnecessary tasks from my routine. But I had already done all of that. I could find no more items to omit from my daily tasks.

On all levels, I more than sensed that I had to implement major change in order to survive. I realized that I could no longer function at the same pace. This was an epic awareness for me. I had needed to get to the point of complete and utter physical, mental, and emotional exhaustion before the biggest lesson walloped me in the face.

> **This lesson** was that I had to "take care of myself first, so I could take care of others".

My personal paradigm shift—the shift in my thinking about who I was now was beginning to occur. My self-image was slowly shifting from that of Musician to Caregiver. This shift created a change in how I approached what I did each day more than what I actually did. It was my first change in the perception of who I was and who John was now. It was the admission and acceptance that there was no going back to our previous life. I realized that our quality of life-style needed redefining.

How to execute this new definition was another issue. I started by taking stock of what I did each day and created a list of items relative to their enjoyment, productivity, and financial gain or drain on my energies. Then I put them in order of most useful at the top and least useful at the bottom.

After a few weeks of personal review, I acknowledged I truly enjoyed working with the computer as an aspect of music synthesis. This was about mid-1993. I knew that computers were the future and there was great potential in that field for creating the financial stability we required. I am grateful and lucky that everything about them was mentally easy for me. A light clicked on in my head. Here was my solution, my salvation. Find a new career in computers.

The next step was figuring out how to create that next career. The criteria for this career became the following in that it must:

- Be financially more lucrative than the minimum wage job at the retail store.
- Provide quality health insurance for both of us.
- Be reasonably close to home, where John was, so I could get there quickly for emergencies.

I knew that finding this career would ease our financial stress. I also knew that the financial stress was wearing down my health and inner reserve faster than anything at this point.

I discovered and took a six-week condensed course in computer network management. The college where I took the course promised "97% job placement success." At the end of the course, I completed the obligatory new résumé and went to the career counselor. Over his lunch at his desk, he explained the only way he could get me a job was if I took an unpaid internship for an unspecified time. It would most likely be for at least six months. That was not a financial option for me so I walked out the door. He was still eating lunch when I left. I later learned that 97% of the people who take the course are already employed in that field. They take the course to upgrade their skills to obtain higher pay. I was the 3% for whom the career counseling department had no intention of providing any service. They did not provide any services to the other 97% either. I felt that the career counseling department was about "eating lunch". So much for Plan A.

Plan B was now in effect. What Plan B was, I had not a clue at that time. I wrote off the over-one-thousand dollars I had paid for the course and moved onward; looking for the next solution.

My research on the current job market taught me that employers like to "try out" an employee as a temporary employee before they hire them. This was part of the unpaid internship concept espoused by the computer school. However, by working through a local temporary agency, I secured a paying temporary job for a research firm. It involved my computer skills and I had about six months there to practice and gain new computer skills.

While at that job in the research firm, my daily car pool partner was the tuba player that had played in our musical group, Rising Winds. He worked across the street at a local university. We had a great time laughing to and from work each day. Serendipitously, an opening occurred in the Music Department in the Music Library. With my car pool partner's recommendation, I interviewed and got the job. I had never been a librarian before, so the job was contingent on my taking a course in librarianship. I found an acceptable course at a community college in another county. I completed the course and was able to keep the job in the Music Library on campus.

This job was another amazing opportunity for both John and me. First, it doubled my previous income. In addition, it provided great health insurance for both of us. Third, John could again come to work with me. He wheeled around the campus, went to the four stories of library and anyplace else he wanted to on campus. It satisfied all of my criteria for my next career!

I gave John money and told him to buy his own lunch. In order to do this, he had to learn how to speak. It forced him to speak. It was either speak or starve. His choice.

He checked into my office throughout the day so I knew he was OK. He had to learn how to work elevators and learn his way around campus. He could also explore the bookstore and student union. I essentially mainstreamed an aphasic stroke victim amongst the safety of a hoard of students, faculty, restaurants, and books. How lucky could we be?

As a result of this opportunity, John made amazing progress with his speech. I snigger today as I realize he really had no choice. Again, gratitude became the mainstay of our lives. We felt gratitude for the opportunity for him to learn, explore, grow, improve, and for me to have stable income with paid retirement and health insurance.

LESSONS LEARNED

The most beautiful aspect of my mental paradigm shift was that it created a totally different set of emotions for me. I was usually too busy to allow anger to settle into my daily emotional soup, but it did creep up now and then. I knew that anger would not serve me in the long run. Anger saps energy and pulls one into victim mode. There was no time to play victim. I knew my philosophy of choosing to take action was the only way to survive and thrive for us. This choice to take action kept my emotions in the love-based realm.

> Whenever anger surfaced for a moment, I merely took notice that it was there. I was aware, but I just let it slide away by thinking of something that I was grateful for at that moment. By choice, I allowed gratitude to replace the anger. I started to feel proud of my ability to take charge of the situation, to make the necessary changes. The changes I was making made the difference in what was occurring in our daily lives. Gratitude is a love-based emotion, as opposed to fear-based emotion. This gratitude allowed me to feel joy in what I was doing.

☙

Every solution I found for me also improved John's quality of life. It helped me be healthier as I was removing layers of stress. Over time I learned that any way I could reduce my stress level was better, not only for me, but also for my relationship with John, and therefore ultimately for him.

I also observed that if John was happy and motivated to keep himself busy with things he enjoyed doing, then I was free to work, take care of the house, and to take care of **me**. It worked both ways.

I realized stress works like a barometer. If my level of it went higher, I could count on the fact that John's ability to cope with his own new lifestyle decreased. If his coping strategy decreased, his stress level rose. If I lowered my stress level, his went down, too. When his stress level went down, it became easier for him to be content with and enjoy his new life. Therefore the solution was to take care of myself better and keep my stress down. That was what allowed me to find more solutions for John and for me. Less stress is really the key.

During these early years of the stroke, my self-care included regular exercise and Jacuzzi time. We all know that exercise relieves stress. For me, the challenge was making myself exercise regularly to help relieve the stress. Carving out time in the week to care for myself in this way was a monumental task. I did not have a gym membership so I jogged around the neighborhood a couple of times a week for many years. Then my treat was to jump in the Jacuzzi when I got home to counteract the physical pain of the jog. During the Jacuzzi time, I would meditate to calm my mind and body. I know this all helped. I would usually sleep better on the exercise/Jacuzzi days.

08

There were also many times when I felt guilty about decisions I made that I learned later were not the best decisions. I did some reading about the life-style changes on the emotional health of Caregivers and learned that guilt is a frequent visitor for the Caregiver. We feel as if we have never done enough, or we have not done it right. Eventually, I embraced the wisdom of knowing, again, that I did what I did during each past moment because it truly was the best I could do at that moment.

Using that awareness and the information that guilt was common for Caregivers, I slowly realized that my guilt was counter-productive. It was hurting me by dragging me down from within.

LESSONS LEARNED

After I realized I had to take care of myself first, I learned two important lessons about how to do that.

First, I learned that "allowing" whatever I did, whatever decision I made, was absolutely perfect for that moment. I based all tasks, ideas, and learning on what I knew at the time. There really is no other way to do it. Looking back at my decisions was not only pointless as I could not change past decisions, but it was also a waste of emotional and mental time. Decisions had been made based on my knowledge during those past moments.

The second important lesson was self-forgiveness and to be non-judgmental about myself. I learned to forgive myself for not only making wrong decisions, but also to forgive myself for the guilt that came with my self-judgment that I had made a "wrong" decision. I learned to let go of the guilt and became free. The best result of self-forgiveness is the freedom that opened up in my mental space to think creatively.

CR

At the point of Caregiver exhaustion: the magic word is "respite".

I kept hearing a word tossed around at John's therapy, in literature, and by not enough people for it to sink into my overwhelmed consciousness for far too long. Finally, I got so exhausted I was near collapse. Another lesson I was meant to learn all along was forced upon me. That lesson was respite. In the world of caregiving, respite is an enigmatic term used to describe a temporary way out from under the Herculean daily tasks of the job. Respite comes in many forms. Sometimes it is an afternoon out, a trip to a day spa, or even something I bravely call a "vacation". Whatever the length of time, it is time spent away from their Survivors, with someone else taking over their duties while they are away.

My biggest problem was that I did not have the financial means to hire help with John so I could experience respite. I was then, and still am the only Caregiver. This caused me to be a great solution finder. Eventually, my employment changed again. Since I was no longer quite as close to home, I was forced to find another solution for some additional help.

Our neighbor, Ellen, was an incredible blessing for both of us. One of the most valuable services she provided over a period of the first ten years we lived in our "new" home was that of respite provider, or someone who watched over John so I could leave the house, and leave town for my own recreation.

Don't Stop the Music

My first full day and overnight away from John occurred nearly three years into the stroke. Jenny, my dear friend, and I decided to take a four day vacation in New Mexico. At the time, she was a database designer for the criminal system of the state in which she lives. Her job was to design and maintain the tracking software for the ankle bracelets of criminals who were not confined to prison. No pressure there. Obviously we both needed time off to recreate and heal our souls.

All kidding aside, the trip away from John cut some very heavy apron strings for me. The first night out, I was shaking in fear because John was home alone. I knew our beloved neighbor, Ellen was next door, but that was slim reassurance when the phone in our hotel room rang at 2:00 a.m. I nearly flew out of my bed and poor Jenny, who had been reading, almost stepped on her jaw as it fell off from watching me fly to the phone. I realized then how "on edge" my nerves and system were after taking care of John with no break for so long. I answered the phone and it was Jenny's husband, calling to say good night to her.

How I long for that to happen with John. Will he ever be able to say "good night" to me? I observe so many other couples our age and watch how they are able to interact with one another. Couples going for a walk in the evening, couples dancing, and couples that can have a real conversation at the next table in restaurant—do they know how wonderfully lucky they are? The pain of these observations is still like a knife in my heart.

Stop thinking about it. I must go on. There is some reason why this path has been chosen for me. Look for the lesson!

That phone call incident was another great lesson for me. We all know that we are supposed to take time off from the pressures of daily life to heal. However, I had not done it for so long, and had been under such extreme pressure for so long that I did not even realize how over the top my nerves were. I had been on 24/7 alert for caregiving and medical emergencies for nearly three years straight. The pressure gradually builds, little by little, and one loses awareness of just how much stress is filling the psyche. This experience taught me that I could not be the best Caregiver if I was this pent up and exhausted. The enemy of fatigue strips us of the ability to take care of ourselves and to take care of the Survivor.

Jenny and I now take this type of vacation periodically, whenever we get to the point of tearing our own hair out of our heads. Our method is to look up "adventure vacations" and then choose our vacation based upon time and price. That first adventure in New Mexico, away from John included horseback riding on the mountaintops. It also included another adventure—visiting the museum at Roswell. Our derrieres paid the price of the riding. Our tongues were firmly placed in our cheeks (the ones on our faces) for the second adventure. If you are unsure of the reason, just type "Roswell" into your favorite Internet search engine.

༄

As I look back at my process of learning to take care of myself first, I realize how slow I was to jump on that bandwagon at each step. I do not feel guilty about that, or judge myself for the seemingly snail's pace. It is just that it was such a huge paradigm shift for me to change from professional freelance-musician-entrepreneur in the music business to that of Caregiver. My previous pace of living easily accommodated the addition of so many new duties in caring for John and being the sole breadwinner for our family. At least that is what I thought. Also, my crystal ball did not tell me that my skills as Caregiver would be needed for so many years. I could not have possibly prepared myself for a totally unknown future. I learned to accept the events of each day and not look forward or back. I began to live in the "now".

The ultimate purpose in sharing my journey is to reveal the wandering path that I took to get to the point of understanding my own process of change in the self-care realm. It happened as slowly as the rhythm of a J.S. Bach "Saraband". My awareness of the need to take care of myself grew over time as I became aware that no one else was responsible for my quality of life. I learned in the most basic way possible, affected by mind-numbing fatigue and persistent experience, that self-reliance or taking responsibility for your own life is evidence of your positive attitude. This positive approach is necessary, always, for Caregivers. I eventually learned to follow the rule: take care of yourself so that you can take care of others. It all works together, one fragment supporting the next, intertwining into the melody of life.

I am incredibly grateful that my physical health has weathered the storm throughout the years without adding health issues for me on top of his. The Universe has given me an astonishing physical constitution. I am grateful each day for my strength. I honor my strength each day with this gratitude.

Part of Each Other

The Tao is a source of peace
for those who need care
and a refuge
for those who give it.
Within the Tao we are not two beings,
forever separate and apart.
We are part of each other
in a manner we cannot truly fathom.
But in the circumstances
that have brought us together,
we feel and know
that this is true.

*We honor ourselves
by caring for others.
We honor others
by caring for ourselves.*

"The Caregiver's Tao Te Ching" by William and Nancy Martin.

Chapter 6

The Survivor's Health

This chapter is devoted to a description of John's health prior to his stroke, or Cerebral Vascular Accident (CVA), during the initial acute phase of the stroke, and up through the present. The purpose of this is to share information that may help others understand and possibly recognize symptoms of stroke and other conditions. Most of the symptom and medical information related here is easily found on the Internet or by asking your doctor. Hopefully, this will help you know what questions to ask your doctor, and what information you should report to your doctor.

As we all know, hindsight is 20/20. If only we could know at the time things are happening that they are a forewarning of things to come. For many years prior to the stroke, John had horrible neck pain that we thought was tension and stress related. As we were not insured when these occurred, we did not seek out medical advice regarding these neck pains. We just attributed these symptoms to "life" and the toll it takes upon all of us.

Knowing what I know now about his diagnosis of Fibromuscular Dysplasia of the Carotid Artery, I am guessing that those neck pains were an early warning of the disease that was building in his carotid artery. Who knew? This is a rare disease, we were told later. Other than that, he was a healthy normal fifty-three year old male.

John had recently acquired health insurance through my employers at the retail store. He had signed up about ninety days prior to the stroke. It was a Health Maintenance Organization (HMO) policy. When he did so, he selected a Primary Care Physician (PCP) from the list in the directory. This doctor was totally unknown to us.

As stated before, John had his stroke in February of 1991 when he was fifty-three years old. For three days prior to his stroke, John was experiencing dizzy spells. It was flu season and everyone was having those same symptoms related to flu. We thought John just had the flu.

Since he had this new health insurance, after a weekend of dizzy spells, I decided to call on Monday morning and make an appointment for John to see his new Primary Care Physician. When I called the doctor's office, I was told that the physician John had chosen was no longer with his health plan and there was no one else in that office that could see him. I was at work, and did not have the opportunity to start searching for a new PCP. He had his stroke Tuesday.

We now know that dizzy spells are often a symptom that a stroke will occur. Please see Appendix I for a link to the American Stroke Association's website where the current warning symptoms of stroke are listed and described.

I wish that I had words to guide everyone regarding symptoms, disease, health care, and prescience, but I do not. I am not a medical professional. All any of us can do is the best that we can, each moment of our lives, based upon the information we have at that moment. That is what I did. Although I wish that I had made different decisions that day, I do not harbor any self-guilt regarding them. Guilt solves nothing and hurts us if we hold on to it. We cannot change the past; we have only the "now". Choosing to maintain this philosophy keeps our brain in positive thinking mode. If we think positive, we have a much better chance of creatively finding solutions to all of life's issues. I learned immediately that my purpose in this chapter of our lives was to find solutions and implement them.

ଓଃ

The first several days of a stroke are called "acute" as this is the time period where the body is still in panic mode and blood pressure is erratic. Continued monitoring of the patient's condition by medical professionals is crucial. I believe I was told by one neurologist that proper medications can slow or prevent further stroke damage if administered quickly. I really do not know about the veracity of this as I am not a medical professional. If a family member is ever having a stroke, make sure to ask the physician about this drug immediately.

When I got to the hospital where John had been taken by ambulance, it is my opinion that the emergency room (ER) team was virtually only monitoring him. I believe they told me they had not received authorization from John's insurance company to treat him. Since I had no prior experience with working with any health insurance, let alone an HMO, I had no idea what any of this meant. While I was talking with one of the nurses, the phone rang, the approval came in, and they rushed to his side to provide full medical treatment. I was standing right there when the phone call came in with the authorization. It is critically important to make sure one knows when these authorizations occur. Write them down, keep notes, and take names.

After the acute phase

Since the hospital where he was at was not the primary hospital for treatment on his insurance plan, once he became stable John was moved to another hospital which was on our insurance plan. It was also closer to our home. Fortunately the hospital to where he was moved is an excellent hospital and he received what I assumed was the best care available.

After he was moved to that second hospital, John was in the main hospital section for about two more weeks while they began minimal occupational, physical, and speech therapy.

Occupational therapy covers anything from the waist up. Physical therapy covers walking, strengthening, and waist down improvement. Speech therapy covers relearning how to speak and may involve additional treatment if the patient has swallowing disorders. I believe I was told that swallowing disorders are common for people with strokes. The explanation is that when one side of the brain is damaged, the opposite half of the body loses its ability to communicate with the brain. Thus all of the internal organs communicate properly on only the unaffected half if they are on both sides of the body. For example, the esophagus frequently loses its ability to coordinate both sides of the swallowing motions.

Another interesting phenomenon of brain damage related to stroke is that vision often disappears on the affected side of the body. I actually saw this symptom in John. When he would eat from a plate, he would eat only the food on the left side of his plate. He could not see the food on the right side of the plate because that was the side of his body that was no longer communicating with his brain. John later told me that one day he woke up and he could see both sides again. His brain swelling had gone down from the stroke and his vision returned. We are both extremely grateful that his vision returned!

૱

After a couple of weeks, John was moved to the rehabilitation unit of this second hospital. It has a reputation of being one of the finest rehab hospitals in Southern California. I was thrilled that John was moving forward with his treatment. While he was in this unit, he was treated with full speech, occupational and physical therapy several times a day. I was phoned daily by the therapists with constant progress reports.

During his two week stay in the rehab unit, John was catheterized. After asking some questions about this, I learned that if the catheter is left in too long, it may end up having to be permanent. I decided this had to change. I asked the nurses what it would take for them to remove the catheter. They gave me an amount that John had to donate to a male portable urinal. It only took about two days to make this happen and as agreed, his catheter was removed. No one wants that for health and human dignity reasons. Neither of us wanted him to be subjected to catheterization for the rest of his life, either.

In John's case, it is my opinion that this catheterization was mostly for the long term convenience on the part of the hospital staff. I believed the nursing staff had no intention of making sure John was able to take care of his own bathroom needs. I state my beliefs because others might find it useful to know that they, the family, may be expected to take care of this re-training of a family member.

Once we had the basic health issues of stabilization and no more catheterization solved, we were able to focus on the recovery issues involved with therapy.

※

In the early days after John's stroke, I was determined that John would recover back to his normal, pre-stroke self. With therapy and hard work, he would recover completely.

Around the three month point in the process, I started learning more about the process of stroke recovery. As I began assessing his potential based upon what I was learning and what I was observing in John's therapy, I realized I had to start creating a new reality as to what amount of recovery was possible.

My new permanent philosophy and methodology for each day became creating the highest and best quality of life for him. This philosophy has now colored all of my decisions since his stroke. This methodology helped me determine what I could do to give John this gift. I needed to think creatively and totally outside of the box to come up with ways to make this happen. I wanted him to be happy and enjoy each day as much as possible while doing what he loved to do.

> Quality of life is the most basic of goals.

Don't Stop the Music

Achieving this quality of life for John became my mission in life. It became my joy.

As the years have passed, John's health has changed in many ways. Blessedly, he has gotten better with his mental acuity. His speech has improved monumentally. He has continued to improve physically as long as he continued to exercise and stay active.

Over time, John has developed high blood pressure and high cholesterol. I do not see this as horribly abnormal nor do I attribute it to the fact that he had a stroke. These conditions are part and parcel of the aging process of life. I do think that they are exacerbated by his relative inactivity due to the results of the stroke. I also know a lot of people who are active and develop these conditions. Fortunately, both are quite easily managed with medications.

John took one drug for a number of years that I believe is popular for the treatment of high cholesterol. According to what I believe I was told by our dentist, is that it has a potentially creeping side effect for some people. This side effect can cause issues with dental health. John has developed nasty problems with his gums. Between the drug use and his inability to brush his teeth as well as he should, he must see his dentist every three months, without fail, to monitor this situation. So far we are grateful we have been able to preserve his teeth.

This is stated here to remind readers that all drugs come with warning sheets that state the potential side effects. I advise that you read them and then work with your licensed medical professional to see if those side effects may be an issue for your loved one. In addition, please note the Legal disclosures presented in the early section of this manuscript.

Solution

Change to a different drug that does not have that side effect. There are many available.

LESSONS LEARNED

Make sure you are aware of the potential side effects of long term use of all medications. Discuss all medications and side effects with the doctors. Ask them for alternative drugs if you have issues with the side effects. Most importantly, read all the warning labels that come with the medications when you purchase them. That small print is very important.

Also, like all of us, if one does not use information, one loses it. I feel that many doctors may be too busy to remain on top of the long list of side effects of every drug. That information is readily available to anyone on the Internet, in periodicals, and also from the pharmacist. Make friends with your pharmacist!

John has two other chronic health issues that require continual maintenance. Neither is related to his stroke. The most serious of these is glaucoma. John has been told that he has only 1.5% of his optic nerve remaining. If you are dealing with this disease, make sure to learn as much as possible about it. What I believe is that glaucoma is a condition of the eye where the fluid in the eye does not drain properly and pressure builds up in the eye. This high pressure destroys the optic nerve over time. The condition is manageable with continued eye drops and other treatments. It is not curable at this time. The eye pressure must be monitored on a regular basis. For John, we still see his glaucoma specialist every three months. Again, I am not a medical professional and my opinions and beliefs are not a substitute for professional medical care.

John's other medical condition that requires continual monitoring is a result of his very fair skin and years of excessive sun exposure. He has recurring bouts with both Basal Cell and Squamous Cell Carcinoma or skin cancer. Most of these are on his face. Over the years he has had many of them removed. Depending upon where they are located and the type of cancer, John has had a type of surgery called Mohs Technique three times. Briefly, it is my opinion that the Mohs surgical technique involves several steps, beginning with the surgeon removing the cancerous area. Next the patient returns to the waiting room, bandaged, and awaits the lab results of the removed tissue. If the outer edges of the skin removed from the surgery are not free from cancer cells, the patient returns to the operating theatre and more tissue is excised. The patient remains in the doctor's office until the surgeon is positive all cancer cells are removed.

Each time John has had Mohs surgery, he has had to return to the surgeon's table at least three times in that day without leaving the doctor's office to have more cancerous tissue excised.

The last time John went in to his very competent Mohs surgeon, John had an episode of extremely high blood pressure after the second trip back into the surgeon's chair. It was so severe that they would not complete the surgery until John was given specific medication to lower his blood pressure. This was more than a little scary. It took a couple of hours. They were afraid John would have another stroke during the surgery. Since I am not a medical professional, it is my opinion that John's fear of the surgery, based upon his past experience, instigated this blood pressure event.

Eventually, the problem was solved and John and I left, much later in the day than anticipated, to return home.

The reason I am sharing this event is that the pressure on the Caregiver for the surgical "after-care" can be quite intense on a Mohs Technique surgery. It depends upon how large the wound is. The Caregiver may be charged with home wound care until the wound is healed and stitches can be removed. This is not for the weak at heart.

For me, it required great diligence on my part to provide sanitary wound care with cleaning and bandaging these wounds to prevent infection. For the first few days, changing bandages occurred several times a day. I chose a time period for the surgery when I, as Caregiver, could be at home for the entire day, for several days, to manage this care.

Solutions for Wound Care

All challenges and worries aside, be at peace and use your head to manage this type of care. It is very doable if one uses good sense and great care to prevent bandages from being soiled prior to applying them.

During this process, I reserve a space where all equipment and supplies can be closed away from children, pets, dust, and from the patient themselves. Make this location convenient to where the Patient will be seated while their wound is being treated. A portable and closeable plastic container works very well. Keep a plastic lined trash can handy for disposing soiled bandages and cleaning swabs.

Thoroughly cleaned hands are an absolute must. Latex or nitrile gloves are another good option.

> Follow all instructions given by the doctor, and keep the doctor's phone number handy. Do not be afraid to call the doctor regarding any questions. Believe me, the doctor and staff would much rather have a call with questions than have a patient back in there with an infected wound that is not healing.

ೞ

Overall, John is in relatively good health and we are both extremely grateful. He has the gene for longevity: his mother passed away a mere four months before her 102nd birthday. His heart is strong, and according to his cardiologist, "he will live forever". John loves to hear these words. He loves life!

I have the utmost respect for John: he awakes cheerful and full of joy almost every day. He wants to live and enjoys every moment. It is truly an amazing thing to watch. His attitude is almost always one of happiness. Of course he has his moments of sadness and irritability, as do we all, but they are rare. On occasion he even wakes up on the wrong side of the bed. If he does, it does not last long. His general happiness may be partially dictated by areas of his brain that were damaged by the stroke. We have no way of knowing. What I observe every day now is that his attitude is not that different from how he was prior to the stroke. His personality is mostly the same.

To the casual observer, he is basically the same person, with a lot of physical and speech limitations.

ଔ

Dealing with brain damage

The most challenging of all of the issues of John's stroke has been the damage it did to his beautiful mind. This incredibly talented musician and composer was instantly felled from a very high level of professional capacity to that of an invalid that could not speak or move, let alone play a trumpet or compose music. It was a very long way to fall. In the flash of a moment, it all disappeared.

I have often described stroke damage to friends by taking a piece of paper, and drawing a circle, or "brain" on it. Then I take a sharp pencil while holding the paper in the air and I quickly punch a lot of holes inside the circle. The imagery invoked by this relatively violent process immediately gives someone a concept of the randomness and vicious damage caused by stroke. Then I explain that as the brain heals, scar tissue is formed where the damage occurred. This process takes about two years. Between the holes in brain and the resulting scar tissue, the brain's ability to send electrical energy to the different areas of the brain is stopped, diverted, changed, and inconsistent. When the electrical energy hits scar tissue, it often causes seizures. John has a seizure disorder and takes medication for it to this day.

No two strokes are alike. Different damage and different levels of damage occurs in each individual depending upon the location in the brain and the severity of the stroke.

Although the damage is different for each individual, there are similarities in stroke damage. For example, John's stroke was in the left hemisphere of his brain. Thus his motor impairment was in the right side of the body. Each hemisphere of the brain controls the opposite side of the human body. Very simply, the left brain controls most logic functions, and the right hemisphere controls the creative aspects of thought. Thus, left brain damage typically causes the loss of language, and right side stroke damages creative thinking and other cognitive skills. Motor skill loss occurs from damage to both hemispheres. The amount of damage in the brain is directly related to the amount of loss of skills. If the brain damage is too severe, the brain can no longer communicate enough with the body to sustain life and the victim dies. This is an extremely simplified description of brain damage from stroke for the purposes of this book.

The impact of the brain damage on someone who has had a stroke is immediate and insidious. In John's case, the stroke in his left brain caused him to lose the use of the right half of his body and all of his language.

I often use the following analogy regarding John's brain damage as a means of helping me maintain compassion for him rather than letting my frustration erupt with his inability to do tasks, remember things, and just function.

> When I was a child I had a bag of marbles. Every spring, it was marble season at my elementary school. We would all start to tote our marbles to school each day to play marbles in the puddles between the melting piles of snow in Minnesota. As I collected more and more marbles from my winnings, there was not room in my marble bag for them all. I started to put only my favorite marbles in the bag with me to take to school each day. Others were left behind at home.

I truly believe that John's brain is similar to my childhood marble bag. He has room only for the thoughts that are most important to him. For example, he remembers to put his trumpet away and where every accoutrement for his trumpet is stored. He cannot, or will not, remember where the extra rolls of toilet paper are stored. This is just one item on a very long list of items that John seems to think he cannot remember. Therefore he expects me to wait on him all day to meet his needs regarding these other items. The items he is able to remember do seem to change intermittently, too. I believe that he chooses his favorite marbles to keep in his bag of memories. I believe this because his personality and memory choices were the same prior to his stroke.

It is my choice to stay in a loving emotional state all day, every day, to meet John's needs. I have learned that I get to choose to make a love-based response to his requests, or a fear-based response of negativity. After years of experience with these issues, I have learned that it is healthier for John and for me, if I make the choice to stay with love-based choices. This does not mean that I allow him to bully me or control my day. As long as I make a choice to serve, it is my loving choice. I can and often do make a choice not to wait on him for everything he requests. The items I choose not to do for him are those that he is totally capable of doing himself. When I make the choice not to serve him, I simply state that I am doing something else and that he can do that on his own.

The emotional intention behind my statement is the significant factor that determines the outcome of the emotional tension in our home. Angry or negative intentions create tension. Loving intentions create no tension. It is my choice to deal with John's brain damage issues with loving intentions at all times.

> One professional in the brain damage field explained that some of John's memory issues may also be a part of what is called automatic memory storage. He may not be making deliberate decisions as to what is important to him. Whether or not he deliberately chooses to remember certain things and not others is most likely immeasurable in scientific or medical terms.

☙

Brain damage also creates the need for the Caregiver to be constantly aware of safety issues around the home. The Caregiver must ever be on guard for safety issues. It is somewhat like babysitting a toddler in that unexpected things can occur that threaten the safety of the stroke survivor. The easiest way I have found to be on "alert" 24/7 is to stay in a state of "love" and not of "fear" in my role as Caregiver on safety alert. Keeping love in the forefront helps me remain calm, able to function, and assists with keeping the fatigue away. This is not rocket science: it is a matter of choice for me. I simply choose "love" by being aware that I can do so.

John is not able to follow instructions because he can only remember the last thing he hears in a sequence of items or sentences. If a waiter asks him whether he wants a baked potato, French fries, rice, or vegetables with his meal, he gets very confused. He can only remember the vegetables because it was the last item on the list. He and I both know he wants French fries but he cannot find that word from the list he heard. That is where his confusion mounts. He knows what he wants, he knows he heard it, but the "vegetables" are stuck in his brain.

An example of this inability to follow instructions involves making a pot of coffee. For years, I could put the water in the coffeemaker, have the ground coffee in the filter, and then have John simply push the start button to make coffee if I was not at home. It was only one instruction. A few years back, I purchased a different style of coffeemaker that does not have a glass pot that is breakable. There is a start button on the front. In addition, this coffeemaker has a unit on the top of the machine that houses the coffee and one simply has to push on a bar with the coffee cup on the front of the machine to have the coffee dispensed directly into a cup being held under the spigot. I felt this style of coffeemaker would be safer for John to use as he could not drop a glass pot and break it. Broken glass is never safe around John. Even after multiple demonstrations of how to fill his cup, he has not been able to learn how to push his cup up against the bar to have the coffee come out of the spigot in the front of the machine.

Recently, I showed him how to turn on this new coffeemaker by pushing the "On" button on the front of the machine. I also showed him again, how to get the coffee out of the spigot by pressing his cup up against the bar. I added the water and ground coffee because I was not going to be home in the morning. I was taking a day of respite and thought he should be able to simply push the button to start the machine. When I arrived home later in the day, he had not made the coffee because he could not find the "On" button directly in front of him. Extremely simple tasks elude him at times. I know this is typical of aphasic people.

It is actually a good thing to have him do simple chores like this. It keeps his brain functioning. Maintaining brain function at even his level is critical to ongoing quality of life issues. Therefore, I keep working at teaching him new household chores that have only one instruction.

Another example of his brain damage and mental incapacity occurs when he is eating. I believe the medical term for this is apraxia. He often has trouble knowing which utensil to use when he is eating a specific food. For example, he will try to eat soup with a fork. Since his left brain or logic side was damaged, these types of tasks often elude him. Sometimes, he will just pick up food with his fingers when it is inappropriate to do so. I have learned to only give him the utensil he needs at the moment to remove his choices.

Here is an amusing example of John's brain damage intervening in the daily affairs around the house. John loves pizza. I always keep a frozen pizza handy for him. One day he asked for pizza so I went to the freezer, knowing I had one there. Much to my surprise there was no pizza there. I did not recall baking that last pizza and was confused. I asked him if he knew where it was. He replied: "oven". I opened the oven door, and there it was, box and all, unopened, sitting in the cold oven. I asked when he had put it there, he said "yesterday". I hope you are laughing. He was trying to be thoughtful and had put it there the day before when he had asked for it the first time. He thought he was helping by showing me he knew where it was to be baked. It never occurred to him to tell me it was there. I had no idea.

These types of events are typical of those perpetrated by folks with brain damage. A good sense of humor is required on the part of the Caregiver. Laughter heals.

Initially, John could do very little around the house. As his brain healed and therapy gave him more motor skills, he could do some household chores. For example he used to be able to empty the dishwasher and put dishes away in the cupboard. As he has aged however, he no longer participates in this type of sharing of household duties. It has been like a bell curve. First nothing, then gradual building of skills, and then as he has aged, his skills are falling off again and he refuses to help in the house at all. I am not sure if it is so much an inability to assist, or unwillingness.

My friends who are familiar with brain damage say this is typical "brain damage" behavior. My friends, who were friends with John's personality before the stroke, feel it is more about the unwillingness. It is all about everyone's opinion of what is occurring in his brain. My vote is still out on this subject.

However, at a certain point in the process, it has become easier for me to just do all of the chores rather than cajole him into helping. I have learned that simplicity in all things is the easiest paradigm shift for me to make. Thus I look for the simplest path to each day's challenges. It is simpler to do the chores myself then to create the angst between us when he either cannot or will not help.

In reality, the challenge with all of these issues is for the Caregiver. It is about finding ways to work around the brain damage, finding yet another solution to create quality of life for both Caregiver and Survivor. It is again about finding the balance between what stimulation is good for the Survivor to keep his brain functioning, and finding the line that he cannot cross regarding doing simple tasks. This is a never-ending task for the Caregiver. This never goes away.

> **LESSONS LEARNED**
>
> While at home, I have learned to give John only the eating utensils he needs rather than confuse him with making choices as to what to use. In restaurants, I simply remove knives, spoons, or forks he will not need.
>
> Simplicity and acceptance of the situation are what creates joy in my life because I actively choose them. Choosing simplicity and accepting the paradigm shift of his diminished capacities is what releases the weight on my shoulders. This release of weight makes my tasks light each day. I have less fatigue, I can live in joy. There is peace in our home.

Brain damage and social issues

What the Caregiver must never forget regarding the care of a stroke survivor is that their brain is damaged. Depending upon the severity of the stroke, they do not process information visually, verbally, spatially, or socially the same way as they did before the stroke. This causes unusual behavior patterns at home and in social situations.

Prior to his stroke, John used to be the life of every party. Some of that skill shows up sometimes in social situations. John is an expert at pretending that he understands what is going on around him. When he knows someone is telling a joke, he has learned to laugh at the appropriate time even if he does not "get" the joke.

Part of not understanding humor is directly related to the aphasia aspect of stroke. It involves many layers of brain function to understand humor in every culture. Over the years I have watched his ability to truly understand humor grow exponentially. He now watches humorous shows on television and laughs from deep within his soul. I believe it is easier for him to understand humor on television than in a social conversation. There is less confrontation because nothing is expected of him from the television.

Sometimes his public misbehavior occurs when we are shopping. Often he wants to purchase something that is unnecessary. If I say, "no, we already have plenty of milk at home", he will start yelling and creating a scene in the store so that he can get what he wants. This is not an uncommon experience. As Caregiver, I have had to learn to diffuse these temper tantrums in public as gracefully as possible. He operates with the emotions, behavior patterns, and desires of a six-year-old child. It is a challenge!

Often when he is in a social situation, an amount of confrontation enters into his aphasia issues. This confrontation occurs because he is in a circumstance where he believes he is expected to react. It is his perception that he is expected to act, or react. This perception on his part is what creates the confrontation. Confrontation shuts down the brain's ability to process multiple layers of information. Because of this issue of confrontation, John has become more and more disinterested in being at social events. It is simply easier to stay home and live out his days as he sees fit. What is comfortable for him is to be at home.

John has created his own beautiful world in his home. He does what he wants and little more each and every day. Because he can do what he wants, without much responsibility to others, he is happy. He is content. I am grateful for his contentment every day. His marble bag is full of **his** favorite marbles. His joy is my joy.

ఇ

The impact of brain damage on the Caregiver lasts forever. The Caregiver spends the rest of their time with the Survivor trying to decipher what the Survivor can and cannot learn or do and must find methods to deal with the issues to create quality of life for both. It is truly all about quality of life. That is the bottom line.

This impact on the Caregiver also goes far deeper than merely discovering things the Survivor can and cannot do. The Caregiver's patience and psychological health is challenged daily by the difficulty of dealing with the brain damage of the Survivor. Compare brain damage issues to the little nagging things that irritate someone in any relationship with another person. Over time, the same issues recur, and recur, and recur. This causes the build-up of tension and stress in a relationship.

To protect my own sanity and quality of life, I know that I have the opportunity to choose how I react to his constant nagging at me for attention and things he needs. He interrupts me every few minutes all day, every day. It took me many years of constant frustration before I made the paradigm shift for myself that I was in control of my reactions to his requests. I get to choose whether or not I comply, teach him to do it himself, or get angry and frustrated. It is that simple. I choose. I have learned to pick my battles so I choose the ones I have a chance at winning. I am also aware that the number of choices I make in this arena on a daily basis is probably more than most people have to make each day.

Even my reaction to that number of daily choices is within my control. I can choose to accept my need to make these choices, and thereby embrace the paradigm shift of our situation. Or, I can choose to resist. Resisting the paradigm shift only hurts me. Believe me, acceptance of a paradigm shift is what brings me to finding the joy in Caregiving.

Overall, the accounts of his health, home participation, and social challenges in this chapter are minor nuisances compared to the similar and often far more difficult challenges of many people in this world. Each day my goal is to provide quality of life, peace, and laughter in our home. We have our moments of discord. Usually they do not last long and end in laughter. We are both aware how wonderfully lucky we are that our days are filled with simple joys, compassion for each other, and love.

Ordinary Caregiving

Some would call it heroic,
a path for extraordinary people.
But Caregiving is really very ordinary.
It is just the Tao expressing itself
in everyday events.

Three virtues
help us along the way:
compassion, simplicity, and patience.
When we have compassion,
we find that fear is gone

and that tenderness replaces toughness.
When we have simplicity,
we find that the need for control is gone
and that generosity takes its place.
When we have patience,
we no longer strive and strain.
Peace becomes our natural experience.

"The Caregiver's Tao Te Ching" by William and Nancy Martin

Chapter 7

The Long Road: Physical and Occupational Therapy

I love learning. The process of learning what therapy was for stroke survivors was fascinating for me. As a teacher and would-be perennial student, learning about the benefits and machinations of occupational, physical, and speech therapy was exciting. I knew it was critical for me to observe John's process and progress from the standpoint of being an advocate for his care. However, once I was able to be at his appointments as much as possible, I got hooked on the process itself. It was as if I was back in college, taking a new class, cracking open a fresh smelling new textbook and diving into a new opportunity to learn something completely different.

Technically, the role of therapy is to reactivate pre-injury neural pathways and thereby restore reintegration and participation in life. The purpose, in lay terms, for stroke patients is to re-train the brain to do normal tasks such as speaking, walking, moving, using the arms, and other cognitive functions, depending upon what areas of the brain were damaged. The entire issue becomes creating the best possible quality of life for the Survivor.

The miracle of therapy is that it can create new neural pathways when the pre-injury pathways are blocked beyond repair. These re-created neural pathways in the brain are used for communication between the brain and the other systems of the body. Voilà, a new neural pathway, and the patient can walk again. Drastically simplified, this is the concept. In practice, it takes a lot of long hard work to create those new neural pathways. Fortunately, the brain is an amazing organ and healing can occur throughout the rest of the life of the stroke victim. Improvement can occur indefinitely, with age related slowing taking a toll as the victim ages.

Looking back at my reaction to learning about therapy, I realize how grateful I am now that I found "Therapy 101" so exciting. My excitement put me on a gratitude ship that allowed me to sail right through the tragedy of why John and I were really in all of these therapy classes. I was able to focus on the goals of his improvement without looking back at the past at all. I locked my panic about John's condition in a footlocker and tucked it away in a musty closet in the hold of the ship. As long as I did not dwell on the panic and fear inside me, I could enjoy my new titles: Chief Advocate and Captain Support during the therapy sessions.

Since I immediately saw the value of "Therapy 101", I insisted that John and I continue as team, as we had for so many years in the music business. We became a "Therapy Team" instead of a musical team, with the new goal of bringing John back to his former life-skills. Our team attitude that was well developed from our music performing careers together kicked in and became the focus of our daily lives for the next two and a half years following John's stroke. I was Chief Advocate and he was the Passenger or Survivor on this cruise.

I believed we would get him back to his former self! If we practiced daily and kept on the same page of the score, he would be walking and talking in no time. All he had to do was pick up the other end of the lifeline I threw to him by getting him to the appointments and working with him at home.

At least this was my plan, this was the theory. I learned many lessons along the way about that plan.

୧୨

Most importantly, I learned that stroke survivors are challenged on so many levels. The condition called Aphasia, the term for the results of brain damage, is an incredibly cruel master of the body and psyche of its victims. Because of the brain damage, their challenge is monumental. For example, in cases like John's where the stroke was massive, it is extremely difficult for them to motivate themselves to do therapy of any kind. His brain was so damaged that all he felt like doing was sitting in a chair and watching the world go by him.

Initially, John's decision making process was non-existent as a part of the aphasia. This is why he needed Captain Support to encourage and insist that he do the therapy that would give him back the part of his life that was so cruelly taken at the moment of the stroke. He was not able to make the decision to help himself.

Fortunately, for the first three weeks after the stroke, John was malleable and just did what his speech, occupational and physical therapists told him to do. He did not have much choice. He was a captive in a rehab unit. His time was managed by the system. His daily schedule was mapped out for him.

After that initial three weeks, my role as Caregiver kicked in and I essentially held the therapy life line out to John. I got to encourage him to pick up that life line. I made the choice to think of my role as something I "got" to do, not something I "had" to do. That simple difference made all the difference in the world for me. I learned that my attitude towards the extra duties I accepted relative to John's progress made it easy for me to be Captain Support. Because I chose to participate and take an active role, it was not a burden to me. My personal fatigue was less because of my personal choice as to how I handled my role. Attitude is everything.

One note of caution here regarding definitions of aphasia and stroke victims: all strokes are different. I am not a medical professional. My understanding is that damage can occur in one area, or it can be spread around like buckshot. It just depends upon the injury itself, and the type of injury. A lot of the initial aphasia is due to the brain swelling immediately after the injury. The brain swells, like any other part of the body when there is injury. Thus the healing of parts of the brain occurs over time as the swelling goes down. As this swelling gradually disappears, many neural-electrical pathways can be reconnected.

Right up front, I was told that much of the brain swelling would be gone at the one month period. The next benchmark is at three months, then six, and then nine months. After approximately two years after the stroke, the swelling is considered completely gone. Because of this healing process, these same benchmarks exist for the benefits from therapy. This is an incredibly complex process. I am not a neurologist and I ask that you educate yourself on this field of medicine if you desire more information.

Because I learned about the swelling/healing benchmarks, I understood that the greatest benefits from therapy occurred within the benchmark windows. The clock ticks. Thus the first month is the most critical time for therapy. The next benchmark becomes the next most critical time for therapy, and so on.

John's choices about therapy came later, when his brain healing reached a point where the aphasia cloud was starting to dissipate. After several months of intensive therapy, he began to be able to conceptualize on his own that there was some success from the therapy and he started to participate in earnest.

I am extremely grateful we had both been teachers for many years. We knew the value of building skills using a variety of tools. As musicians, we both subscribed to a method of "practice, practice, practice". These were and are the methods we used then and the methods we still use—tools and practice.

☙

The actual process of physical and occupational therapy for John began immediately after the acute phase of his stroke was over. The PT and OT in the second hospital each did a Clinical Assessment of his current condition and developed a series of exercises to begin the process of healing for him. I do not know what they did at the second hospital before he was moved to the rehab unit of that hospital as I was not there.

For the two weeks he was in the rehab unit, I received regular calls from the therapists that gave me a report of his progress. Again, I could not observe his therapy because I was at work at the retail store six days a week, solving our financial issues.

The real therapy-in-earnest began when John was moved back home at just over two months after the stroke. This occurred when the insurance effectively said "we have done all we will do" at this time. It now became our responsibility to continue.

Hints for occupational therapy

"Team Therapy" now developed a routine at home by hiring Kaley as our private therapist to come to our home weekly for OT. In our home she continued the process she had begun in the SNF. She worked on posture and retraining his right arm by doing weight bearing exercises and increasing all aspects of static and dynamic balance.

The new goal was a 50% to 50% ratio in which John was to actively participate in 50% of the process for all Activities of Daily Living, or ADLs, while the Caregiver did the other 50% of the work. This means, for example, that John would be able to move an arm toward a sleeve of a shirt and get the arm into the sleeve. Other ADL skills such as dressing, mobility, eating, bathing, and transferring to and from a wheelchair were part of this process.

On the days that Kaley was not at our home, John and I worked feverishly against the ticking clock on our own. We established a routine to continue to rebuild neural pathways on a daily basis. We practiced what we learned from Kaley and made up a lot of games on our own that kept the fun factor in our lives. We purchased therapy tools and used them regularly.

One of the tools we purchased was an over-the-door pulley device. It was positioned over a closet door in his practice studio where he played his trumpet daily. A rope was strung through the pulley that had a hand grip on one end and a bean bag weight on the other. John's task was to pull on the hand grip for a specified number of repetitions or "reps" each day to strengthen his now paralyzed right arm. The purpose was intended with a three-fold outcome. One was to keep his shoulder loose so it would not lock and another was to work the muscles in his arm to hopefully build them to a point where he could move the arm again. The beauty of this system was that as the bean bag pulled his arm back up, the brain received feedback from the arm regarding how it "felt" to move "up". That was the third outcome. John worked on this for a number of years but was never able to gain enough movement back in the arm for it to be of any use for him. He eventually gave up on this exercise because he saw no improvement.

Two purchases we made helped both of us. The most fun item was an adult tricycle where the seat was actually a molded plastic chair seat. The unique frame of this tricycle was open on one side where John could walk into the frame, sit down, and then we would use Ace brand bandage elastic wrap bands to tie his right foot to the right pedal, and his right arm to the handlebars. We were able to use this tricycle for a number of years. It was fun for us because I was able to do my morning jog alongside him and keep myself in better shape while I was assisting his therapy. This morning fun helped strengthen his legs and it helped with maintaining some flexibility in his right arm. In both cases the left leg and arm created movement for the right leg and arm. The right leg and arm then sent messages back to the brain with the hopes that he could develop new neural pathways in the brain to increase the movement in his right leg, and regain movement in his right arm. This tricycle was useful for both PT (legs) and OT (arms). He used this tool for many years but did not regain any movement in his right arm.

The other purchase we made that was intended to help both of us was a stationery workout machine that moved legs, arms and torso, and was designed to be a more full body workout. We both used it in our living room until John developed severe pulled muscle reactions to the style of the workout. He was having his stronger left side do all of the work instead of encouraging the weaker right side to participate. Thus he got severe pain in his left side from overworking it. Our best laid plans for that machine did not assist either of us in the long run. We eventually donated that machine to a local thrift store.

Hints for physical therapy

For physical therapy, we hired a private therapist who worked in a hospital in a nearby city. She had permission from the hospital to bring private patients into the hospital gym prior to the hospital therapy hours. Thus we arrived at this hospital at 7:15 a.m. three days a week for a one hour session. John worked out in that amazing facility with a top-of-the-line NDT Therapist for over a year.

This physical therapist worked mostly on John's "gait" or his ability to walk correctly. Since he had been taught a different gait in the SNF, she was re-training his muscles to work in a normal walking gait. I watched him walk with a totally normal gait during his therapy sessions for longer and longer periods of time.

One interesting situation arose while John was working with the NDT therapist in the hospital. Although he was perfectly capable of walking with a normal gait, the moment the therapist said "We're done for the day", John would immediately revert to the incorrect gait he had learned in the SNF. I asked the therapist about this and I believe her reply was "He learned the other gait first, so it feels normal and more comfortable for him." John truly was not interested in relearning a new way of walking so I discontinued paying for that therapy. He made the physical and emotional choice. I made the financial choice because of his choices.

CR

A device we purchased for PT work at home was a set of bicycle pedals that connected to the front of a chair. He could sit on the chair and pedal in the house to strengthen his legs. The intention was to build-up his partially paralyzed right leg muscles so that they would help with his walking gait. Again, a multi-purpose outcome was hoped for, but did not materialize.

All of this private therapy and the purchases we made for home equipment were paid for from monies donated by the benefit put on in John's honor by our musician friends. None of this private therapy would have happened without that donated money from our musician colleagues. We are extremely grateful to them.

CR

LESSONS LEARNED

Caregivers must make decisions regarding the continuation or discontinuation of a specific therapy modality using several criteria. First, make sure the therapist is actually helping the patient progress in their skills. Some discussion with the therapist regarding the progress of the patient may be helpful.

The second thing to consider is whether or not the resources to pay for this therapy are in place. Whether it is insurance or private payment, the therapists deserve to be paid properly.

The third consideration is the expenditure of time and energy by the Caregiver and Survivor. If there is no progress, or if there is no way to pay for the therapy, then the time invested is not worth it.

Hints for when to cease regular therapy

The decision boils down to, when is enough, enough?

There is no definite answer for the Caregiver and Survivor as to when "enough is enough" in the long road of therapy. There may always be improvement that can be gained from therapy, or the amount of damage in the brain may limit the amount of potential improvement.

Defining criteria for success with therapy is a challenge for all members of the Therapy Team. From the therapist's point of view, the patient's goals are central to the amount and type of therapy offered and given.

I believe that if the patient is mentally competent, they should be included in this decision to continue or stop therapy. However, if the patient is not able to make decisions regarding their own care, these decisions must be made by the Caregiver. All sorts of emotional and guilt issues may arise for the Caregiver when having to make these decisions.

The stroke Survivor's criteria is the most difficult to define because someone with severe aphasia may not be able to put together their own desires in their mind. In addition, the aphasia condition itself dis-allows the Survivor's ability to describe to the other members of the team, what they wish for themselves if they even know what they desire. They may or may not be capable of understanding therapy improvement, goals for therapy, or goals for their own future well-being. The variables are endless based upon the severity of the brain damage.

In regards to these criteria, the biggest issue for the Caregiver to remember is that the better quality of life you can provide for the Survivor, the better your own quality of life will be in the future. It is a two-way street. The more the Survivor can do for themselves, the less you will get to do to serve them. It is most certainly to the advantage of the Caregiver to encourage, assist, cajole, or whatever it takes to insist upon the continued therapy for the Survivor. Their success is your success! Moving towards the ratio goal of 100% to 0% is the ideal. That means that the Survivor is totally self-sufficient and the Caregiver is no longer needed in their role as Caregiver.

For me as Caregiver, my initial criterion for success was getting John back to his former self. Using my past perfectionist ethic that was carefully developed in my career as a professional musician, I envisioned nothing less than a full recovery for John. As we moved past the first year of therapy and into the second full year and beyond, my criteria for success had to adjust based upon the reality of what was actually possible.

The way I made decisions was to make the criteria firmly based on creating the best possible quality of life for John. I also looked at the amount of financial output relative to the amount of gain during the therapy sessions. After the big push of the first year's benchmark,

I observed even more carefully what was occurring in the therapy sessions. I made decisions based upon the modality and method used by the therapists. If it appeared to me that John was making progress with a therapist, I continued paying for the therapy. If the therapist seemed to be treading water and not adding new tasks, the first thing I did was find another therapist. Often a simple change in the personality of the therapist helped John become interested in improving again. It became more and more critical for me to observe the therapy sessions in order to assess progress towards a higher quality of life for John. I never forgot that the higher his skills became, the easier my role would be in the future.

At the decision point regarding ceasing therapy, it is critical for the Caregiver to remember that decisions can only be based upon the information you have at that moment. If the decision is based upon a loving approach towards oneself regarding the amount of resources expended by the Caregiver, then that is the best possible decision that can be made.

※

There was one fear regarding therapy still nagging at me, pinching me in the middle of the night and keeping me from sleeping. It kept creeping around the house like a dark specter. It lurked in all the corners of my mind. This fear resulted from the fact that I knew John's personality so very well. I knew that John had always been a person who thrived on instant gratification on anything that did not involve music. With the music skills of performing or composing, John was more focused than any human I knew. With everything else, like a typical artistic personality, John was truly uninterested. He lived for music only. All other aspects of life either resolved themselves instantly or he allowed them to slip aside and he simply refused to participate. Thus his musical personality had its own catch-22. He knew the benefits of practice and work, but since therapy was outside his work ethic with his music, I feared he would lose interest.

As we embarked on the therapy train, starting slowly and gradually building skills, I knew that once John's brain healed more, his true personality would return. Initially, his personality was shrouded in the haze of severe aphasia. With trepidation, I felt that as he healed and the shroud slipped away, he would lose interest in working on therapy. This was the dark specter of fear that lived in me. I knew that the window of time we had to make great progress before his attitude shift occurred was precious.

This fear motivated me to become Super Caregiver. I wanted to polish that window of time until it sparkled. My dogged insistence on all-the-therapy-we-could-squeeze-into-every-minute-of-every-day became fanatical. There was not a moment to waste.

Then one day, at about two and a half years into the intense therapy, my fear became reality. John informed me he truly believed that he would wake up one morning and he would be able to walk again, and his right arm would function normally. He thought he did not have to "do" anything to make this happen. His words were closer to "wake up, fine!" But I knew what he really meant. He had made a decision to stop working at therapy. We crashed into the wall of no return regarding his cooperation with the therapy.

LESSON LEARNED

Typically the personality of the Survivor eventually kicks in and they know what they can and cannot do. They then decide whether they will continue therapy to earn more skills, or if they are content with requiring that the Caregiver do certain things for them. This can become a contentious point for Survivor and Caregiver. The Caregiver's most important criterion for skill building must always be to consider safety of the Survivor first. Past that point, the Caregiver gets to choose how much they are willing to do for the Survivor, and whether or not additional help must be hired in the home.

◯℞

After about three years, John was no longer involved in regular therapy. He was able to walk around the house, slowly, using chairs, walls, and doors as support or for points of balance. He went for a walk each day, wearing his leg brace and using his cane, halfway around the block and back to the house. During that time he also bathed himself daily and got himself dressed. He helped in the house by doing his own laundry and taking clean dishes out of the dishwasher and putting them away. Often he helped clean the cat litter with his one good arm. It goes without saying that he practiced his trumpet and wrote music for two to three hours daily. All of this was accomplished using only his left arm as his right arm has remained paralyzed and was now frozen in a bent position. In my opinion, he had reached the 85% to 15% ratio regarding his ability to help himself. This meant he contributed 85% of the work, and the Caregiver contribution was at 15%.

☙

As the years passed, Team Therapy took advantage of the maximum amount of therapy that Medicare would cover each year. It varied by year, but for about eight to ten years, almost every year, John went to a local physical therapy gym and worked with a therapist for six to eight weeks, one or two times a week. Again, it depended upon how much was covered by Medicare. During this time of muscle strengthening each year, I noticed improvement in his walking, his energy level, and his mental acuity. I am not sure if he was aware of how much better he got by this work. I kept telling him how well he was doing as a means of encouragement. He knew I was willing to schedule sessions and drive him to and from those appointments for as long as he wanted. By about twelve years into that routine, John tired of that work and he refused to attend any more sessions. He determined what his criteria were for the quality of his life.

☙

As many more years have passed, and John is now in his middle seventies, he spends less time on the trumpet and writing music each day. He has brought it down to one hour at each task. He needs assistance getting in and out of the bathtub. It is also more difficult to get clothing on his upper body as the frozen position of his right arm inhibits his ease of dressing himself. I get to assist with dressing more and more often. He no longer takes his outdoor walk unless I go with him. He does not help with any household chores. However he is happy and content with his life.

I get to be of service as I am needed because I have arranged my work so that I may work from home most of the time. This makes me available whenever he asks for help. I live in gratitude that I have the flexibility to be at home with him and manage his care. Team Therapy made the paradigm shift to accept the outcomes of our early work, and created a joyful life based upon the success of what John achieved. Because we do not look back to our previous life, our joy comes from knowing that we achieved the best possible outcome.

Laughter abounds in our home as we enjoy each day together.

Remain Behind

*When caring for others,
remain behind them.
Help them,
but do not control them.
Serve them,
but do not manipulate them.
Attend them,
but do not diminish them.*

*The river of the Tao
runs through them.
Stay out of the way,
and let that river do its work.*

"The Caregiver's Tao Te Ching" by William and Nancy Martin

Chapter 8

Silent No More: Re-learning to Speak

The gift of speech for humans is the most common method of communication between us. It is part of the universal need to connect with one another. No matter what language is used, communication is the goal. Communication within one's own mind is the quintessential necessity for the formulation and use of language. If one's own thoughts are muddled because their brain is damaged, the ability to communicate outwardly is almost impossible. It requires incredible tenacity and courage to reassemble language in the brain damaged by stroke.

As a result of his stroke, John was unable to speak. His brain was so damaged that it could not find any words to match his thoughts. My understanding of what happened is that the damage in the left side of his brain left holes over which the electronic network of neurons could not hop. The bridges in the electronic freeway in his brain had been broken. The cars or electrical neurons could not get from point A to point B. The travelling neurons could not retrieve the information they needed.

In addition, John's decision-making process was non-existent as a part of the aphasia. The loss of language from aphasia causes the patient to be unable to put together concepts, make decisions, or anything relative to internal or external communication. It is my understanding that internal communication refers to the brain's ability to communicate within itself in addition to an ability to think clearly. External communication refers to the ability to communicate what thoughts exist to anyone else. John lost his ability to rationally look at issues and make decisions. He was merely an observer in the process of life. Initially, he was not able to understand the concept of therapy relative to its potential for him.

This often becomes one of the biggest challenges for the Caregiver: motivating the Survivor and getting them to understand the value of therapy. Then the Caregiver has to get the Survivor to participate in therapy when it is so difficult for them at the moment. The aphasic brain can be like meandering through a gray mist of lost neural pathways. The Survivor may feel lost in a world of nothingness, and the Caregiver's challenge is to understand how lost they feel. Concepts that the Caregiver feels are so obvious and reasonable may not be accessible to the Survivor. Then the Caregiver must find a way to reach into that gray mist and help the Survivor want to free themselves from their prison.

I feel it is particularly challenging in the speech arena for any therapy team. As John's Caregiver, I was extremely fortunate in that he really wanted to speak again. John wanted to learn. He was hungry for his voice again. Each Caregiver and Survivor must find their own way, their own path, and develop their own goals for the quality of life that they want to achieve. All I can suggest is that the Caregiver and Survivor adopt William Churchill's motto: "Never, never, never give up!"

Let me clarify that John's initial ability to speak after his stroke consisted of two curse words only for the first six months. There is no need to repeat them here, but that is all he could do. John shouted them as his method of saying anything and as an attention getting device if he needed something. These words were not at all connected to what he wanted or what he wanted to say.

I believe I was told by speech therapists that the part of the brain that stores curse or swear words (those words that have inappropriate negative connotations in any culture) are stored in a different area of the brain. Apparently that area is rarely affected by stroke. The brain is so desperate to communicate anything that it spits out the only words it can find: cursing and swearing. This is why a stroll down the hallways of most nursing homes finds one's ears burning with the pathetic attempts at communication by the inmates. I call them inmates because they are indeed in prison, usually the prison of their own brain.

John is expressive aphasic. Specifically, John is affected by Broca's Aphasia. This means he understands most of what is going on, but cannot speak back to reply or interact with what he hears accurately. I am explaining this as a lay person, not as a medical professional. His condition is similar to our struggle to find a word that is "on the tip of our tongue" but we cannot remember the word we want to say. I cannot even imagine the level of confusion and frustration he must have felt then, and what he still feels, although it is to a lesser degree.

Also, as I have learned, strokes affect each person differently, there are no rules as to what they can and cannot do. There are commonalities and patterns, but not rules. It all depends upon which areas of the brain were damaged by the stroke. Some stroke survivors also lose their ability to enunciate specific words or sounds. Their control of the actual movement of the vocal chords, tongue, and oral cavity are compromised. This issue was only a small part of John's speech issue. John lost language itself.

Because he had lost his language, he could not write words either. I made an immediate decision to help him first regain his most preferred language, that of music. I knew that his brain would grasp that language before he would re-learn anything else because that was the language of his soul.

Speech therapy John and I did together

To develop the critical skills necessary to learn language, I became a regular at major toy stores in the area. The first item I purchased was a toy called a Magna Doodle®, made by Fisher Price. It was a device that was a tablet shape that contained magnetic filings inside. John could draw on it with magnets or a stylus. The first thing I did, the day after he arrived in the second hospital was draw a musical staff of five lines on it with the stylus. I also drew a musical treble clef sign and handed him the round magnets. He immediately started creating musical "notes" on the staff. My heart leapt for joy! He was aware of what was going on and knew how to create music! This was a starting point for relearning how to write music and to learn the visual skills he would need to learn to speak again.

I continued looking for items or games that we could do together to help redevelop skills in his brain that I knew were critical for him to re-learn how to speak. We were both determined that he would not stay in this condition. My purchases included sets of colored markers, flash cards of letters, words, and math, and many of the language and math workbooks for kindergarten through 3rd grade learners. I purchased computer games, and battery operated word games.

Later on in this process, the speech therapists told me it was not a good idea to use children's items with an adult at the risk of offending their dignity. I disagreed.

My disagreement was on two levels. First, I could not find the type of learning tools I wanted in adult versions. Second, John is an avid toy collector. He was digging this opportunity to play with toys again.

Our daily work from day five of the stroke included continual practice drawing pictures and writing music with the Magna Doodle®. I was working on re-learning spatial concepts. We played games. One of the games was for me to draw half of a simple item. John was charged with drawing the other half and completing the item. I would draw half of a tree. John had to complete the tree. In order to do that, he had to recognize what the half-item was that I was drawing and then he had to reach into the creative area of his brain and practice drawing with his left hand. Prior to the stroke, John was right-handed: he was also dealing with learning to use his left hand to draw and write.

The skill to do this involves more than simply drawing the lines. This involved spatial concepts of matching the other half of the tree, and making the tree he drew fit on the Magna Doodle®. Below is a list of skills required to draw the other half of an image that I have created from my understanding of brain function. I am not a medical professional but I learned the following from spending hours with John, trying to find solutions to his learning problems.

Brain communication requires:

1. That the two hemispheres of his brain communicate with each other.
2. That both the left hemisphere, which is mostly logical, and the right hemisphere, which is mostly creative, recognize what the half-item was.
3. That once recognition occurs, that the brain be able to assemble the correct commands to tell the hand to create the other half of the drawing.
4. That the brain be able to recall the set of commands and actually DO them. I learned that these are two separate tasks for the brain. Brain damage frequently breaks that internal communication link between RECALL and DOING.

In addition to drawing the items with the Magna Doodle®, I would talk about what the drawn item was, say its name, and let him reconnect the neurons of his brain by constant stimulation with words. As he advanced in his concepts, we wrote his name, my name, and other words. We worked on the alphabet. He learned how to read the numbers again.

After about a year of this work together, I managed to buy an inexpensive older computer for John to use. I bought software that included concentration type games, word games, and other educational tools. These not only entertained John, but helped him develop skills he needed to begin speaking again. He played one "concentration" style game for hours. His task was to match pictures on a grid that were the same and hopefully develop his short term memory. As he advanced, it gradually went from a game of 9 tiles, to 15, to 24, and so on.

Amusingly enough, one day I watched him do a more advanced level of this game. He had discovered that if he selected the upper most tile on the left, and then systematically went from the next tile to the right, and then the next, and then the next, and then to the next row, he would eventually find all of the matched tiles. I roared in laughter. He had found a way to beat the game. For me, I was thrilled because his brain had gone past guessing and into problem solving mode. This was a quantum leap forward for an aphasic person. What joy!

Another simple therapy exercise I devised after John was able to say some words again, was to put sticky notes on nearly everything on the house. Each sticky had the word "refrigerator", "doorway", "bathroom", "bedroom", "piano", "chair", "front door", naming the item. I did this on whatever I could find a spot to put on a sticky. That way when John was moving about the house, it was his task to say the name of the item he was passing. This was to re-acquaint him with the names of items. He enjoyed it. This task gave him the opportunity to practice almost constantly in the house.

All of the tasks described above were things John and I did in addition to the therapy that was provided by the insurance company. Our teamwork was constant. Every spare moment turned into a lesson of some kind. We got extremely creative and laughed as much as possible over how silly we had become. We had our own private joy while he was rewiring his brain for language because it involved what we knew as musicians—practice, practice, practice!

> In the twenty five years that have passed since John's stroke, the amount of easily accessible language relearning tools for adults has skyrocketed. I truly wish that I would have had the many tools that are now easily available to anyone who can access Amazon.com. Simply use a computer, go to the Amazon website, and use the search terms "aphasia and speech". Over one hundred pages of products will pop up and be at your fingertips. All of these are available for you to work at home with your Survivor, and assist with their speech recovery.
>
> The real blessing of Amazon.com, is that you do not have to live near a major population center to have access to their service. The tools will be delivered to your door!

Speech therapy with professional therapists

The job of a Speech Therapist is to retrain speaking ability and the cognitive functions related to communication. They do this by rebuilding the original neural network pathways of information retrieval. It is also about retraining the brain to use different areas of the brain and create new neural pathways for the information. It is essentially building new plumbing through which the information travels. The technical term for the brain's ability to change and heal itself is *neuroplasticity.*

John began his regimen of speech therapy with professionals about ten days after his stroke, five days after he and I had already started our daily work. It occurred at the second hospital in the stabilization unit prior to his move to the rehabilitation ward. Since I was working during the day, I visited him before I went to work and again after work. I was not an observer in this initial therapy process because it happened in the middle of the day. I did get a call every two to three days from the therapist with a report on what his prognosis was.

I wish that this first therapist could have a conversation with John today. If the prediction of his only being able to learn 150 words was meant to discourage or prepare a family for living with someone who would forever live only in their own mind, unable to communicate, I disagree with the methodology. Fortunately, it worked exactly the opposite for us. I was determined, with John's help, to never let that happen to him. He would learn to speak again.

Once he was moved to the rehabilitation unit of the second hospital, he received daily speech therapy. Again,

I was not there, so I did not know what was happening in these sessions. The reports from the therapists continued every two to three days.

When John was transferred to the Skilled Nursing Facility (SNF), I began doing actual research on speech therapy myself. I did this in libraries and by asking others in the field about where I could get materials. Most did not give me any help. Either they did not know where I could get professional level materials, or they were unwilling to give me the information. As noted in other chapters, the therapy that occurred at the SNF was woefully inadequate.

It was when John came home, about eight weeks after the stroke that the intensive speech therapy began. Our Occupational Therapist, Kaley, was a wealth of information. Because she was at the high end of the therapy circles in the Los Angeles medical community, she was able to assist us in finding superb private speech therapists that would come to our home. Using funds donated by a family member, I immediately hired a speech therapist that Kaley recommended, to come into our home two times a week.

This recommended speech therapist would come for an hour and work with John at the dining room table. I was always there when this was happening. Although I was usually teaching a private music student at the time, I could still observe and learn from what the therapist was doing. I was soaking up the techniques of what they did. They always gave John homework to do in the days in between sessions. I helped with his homework and spent time with John daily to retrain his brain. I added that help to the daily therapy he and I already did on our own.

Speech therapy with professionals continued with a two-or-three-times-a-week regimen for two and a half years. We changed therapists as one moved away or we found someone else who was better. The final days of professional therapy were with a gal who specialized in conversational style therapy. She and John just sat and talked to each other. Her homework packets were quite intense in that she encouraged working on sentence structure. John was already way past the one hundred and fifty word prediction. His tenacity and desire coupled with the team of people that worked with him daily has created a true miracle.

ᛕ

For several months John saw a Chinese Acupuncturist that specialized in treating stroke patients. I wish that we had known about this treatment sooner. In China, I was told they treat stroke very effectively if done within the first month when the most healing occurs. We did this at about the two year point. The interesting thing is that immediately after his treatment when we were driving home, John suddenly spoke with normal speech patterns and vocabulary for about thirty minutes. We stopped that therapy when I realized that the speech gained from the money spent was temporary. If you want to try this type of therapy, do it within thirty days of the stroke and make sure you find an acupuncturist that specializes in stroke treatment. Apparently it is a high level specialty. I recommend that one does one's research on this alternative method of therapy.

☙

John could still read. He made a conscious choice to develop his brain through reading. Our home has always been filled with books. Since he had already read most of those at home, over the years John has spent countless hours in the local libraries. While there he initially read large print books and then moved to regular print and magazines. He particularly enjoys reading all the back issues of magazines. He started at the beginning of "Life" magazine and read all of the issues. He still attributes this time in the library as one of his strongest self-motivated practices of relearning language. He has told me that initially his comprehension was weak but over the years it has improved to amazing heights. There are no limits to his interest or personal intention to learn. Libraries are free in this country. What a gift to everyone.

Speech Therapy Solutions that do not Cost Much

I bought a large mirror and put it in an old frame that we had at home. It was in front of John on the table so he could watch himself speaking. The visual aspect of this helps the brain learn.

I put a candle in front of him and required that he blow it out, over and over again. This strengthened his ability to push air through his mouth. When he started playing his trumpet again, it also helped immensely with this task.

I bought John countless workbooks of beginning language skills and helped him do the assignments. The phonics approach of many of these helped him relearn the organization of language.

When we were driving to therapy appointments, we sang simple folk songs together. Stroke patients can frequently sing because that skill is stored in a different part of the brain. He relearned the words of the songs.

Another game during driving was this: I would "write" a word on the dashboard. I was really just tracing it and it was invisible. John's job was to discover and say what I was writing. This helped John to mentally watch what I was writing, retain each letter in his head, and then assemble the word. He got very good at this.

> I bought a battery operated child's toy game that was designed to teach spelling. Those types of tools are far more sophisticated now than they were in the early 1990's. I suggest seeking them out.
>
> The best practice of all: simply keep talking to your Survivor. It is about conversation, and enjoying the time you spend together. If the loss of language was severe, over time, the Caregiver will learn to understand the Survivor's little speech patterns that he or she develops.

To date, John speaks and can hold conversations to a certain degree. His best conversations are about music, as that is the corner of language that is most familiar to him. He tells me about the books he is reading. He tries to order food in a restaurant. One of the tricks I learned early on with him, and still use, is "cueing" his words. I will say "John, look at me" and then I will mouth, silently, the word he is trying to retrieve. When he sees me, he reads my lips and then can say what I am mouthing. It is a good thing I usually know what he wants to say.

The Man in the Mall

One day about two years after his stroke, John and I were wheeling through a local shopping mall. Another man, about John's age, was in a wheelchair and his Caregiver was sitting on a bench. Both were watching people.

John wheeled over and haltingly said "HELLO, What's by you?" That is John's way of saying "How are you?" The man and the woman were flabbergasted. The woman said, "He can speak?" She and I began a conversation, and the other man had tears in his eyes. He was trapped in his mind and could not utter a word. Their health insurance had sent him home shortly after his stroke, and no one ever told them that they could get therapy or work on their own to rebuild his skills. I briefly explained how John and I had worked on our own in addition to having private speech therapy in our home.

My heart was broken for this man and his Caregiver. To this day I get tears in my eyes whenever I think of these beautiful people, trapped in the inability to speak to one another. I know all too well the loss of language. I cannot even imagine the level of frustration that accompanied each moment of their lives.

The serendipity in meeting this man in the shopping mall was that we realized yet again that life is what you make of it. This is not a judgment against that man and his Caregiver. They were in a different place.

This was an awareness of how truly blessed John and I were in taking the approach of keeping a good attitude, choosing to take action, and as a result, we are grateful

> for our success. We created a set of tools we could use to bring a high level of quality of life back to John. It is all about taking responsibility for your own life. John succeeded to a level way beyond all expectations, with the help of a Caregiver who believed in him.

Our communication with each other now is based upon over thirty years of friendship. Our inability to understand each other at times is the cause of most of the frustration in our daily lives. Most often, I can figure out what John is trying to say when he gets stuck. We all have this happen. It is like having a word on the "tip of our tongue" and not being able to retrieve it. This "stuck-ness" is difficult on both of us. I get to spend time daily trying to decipher some aspect of speech with him. His frustration and mine does build to the point where one of us will finally say, "let's figure this out later." We usually do figure it out. Sometimes we do not.

That is when both of us take advantage of another gift: the art of "letting go". We have learned to let go of that particular conversation and the frustration that goes along with it.

The peace that arrives after we let go is a beautiful reminder that words are only one way to communicate. More importantly, sometimes words are not needed at all. It is just the joy of two people living together, being at peace in the wisdom that who we are as a team is far more important than whatever words were not spoken that day.

ଔ

The brain is such an amazing and fragile organ. Once damaged, it attempts to retrain other areas of itself to do necessary tasks. New research on the brain's ability to heal is occurring at breakneck speed. Educating yourself about the possibilities is inspiring for both the Caregiver and Survivor. Please see the Resources for Caregivers and Survivors Appendix.

Stroke survival is not a solo venture: it is about the Survivor and the Caregiver, gracefully dancing together to their own music, seeking joy together. Hopefully the couple in the Mall found it. I know we have.

Trust the Tao

Medical diagnoses and prognoses
create the illusion of predictability
and control.
Life's mysteries are too subtle
for prediction and control.

Medical knowledge may be helpful,
but it is not the substance of your caring.
Beneath the knowledge lies this truth:
All forms arise from the Tao,

Nancy Weckwerth

live in the Tao,
and return to the Tao.

Use your knowledge,
but trust the Tao
for the arising, living, and returning.

"The Caregiver's Tao Te Ching" by William and Nancy Martin

Chapter 9

Socializing Again: The Joy of Forgiveness

When John had his stroke in 1991, I was totally unprepared for so many aspects of his condition. One of the most upsetting results was the gradual fading away of our friendships with others. I recall the days, months, and years after my seventeen-year-old brother passed away in a freakish car accident in 1975. Immediately after the death, there were tons of family and friends who were there, supportive, and sending condolences via cards. Then, by about two weeks after the funeral, that sort of support began to dwindle for myself and for my distraught parents. By six to eight months later, I realized that although our immediate family's grief was still raw, the grief of extended family and friends had begun to fade. The grief of others, since they were not immediate family members, fades much more quickly. This was an interesting lesson for me.

Thus, when John had his stroke, and our friends started to disappear, I realized it was the same phenomenon. John and I dealt with the catastrophe on a daily basis, but the lives of those around us, went on. Their music gigs continued, their lives moved forward in the same direction. The social and business lives of musicians are only as active as the next performance. Once you are no longer on the job, or gig, as they are called, your name gets shuffled aside.

There were a few friends who hung in with John and visited with him in the SNF. I particularly recall a tuba player, who was a close friend of John's, who came often to visit John in the Skilled Nursing Facility where he was for about thirty days after the stroke.

As John's time in the SNF ended, the regular visits of most of his friends stopped entirely. I expected this and was not hurt by this at all. Their lives moved forward: everyone is ridiculously busy. We were ridiculously busy working on getting John to recover! I, myself, have been guilty of not visiting friends who have lost loved ones as often as I realize they might need it.

All of our close family members lived thousands of miles away so their lives continued on their own paths. The day by day events in our lives were not even visible to them. It was really not feasible for John's elderly relatives to get on a plane and travel to visit. This is the price we paid for choosing to have a career in the music business, our heart's desire, which took us far away from close family. Our lives as professional musicians called us to major cities where there were jobs for us.

We always accepted the trade-off of profession versus being near to close family members. It was not even an issue for us. We made the choice that was right for us: we followed our dreams.

There were a few other friends who were more than helpful for many months. Some came and mowed our lawn when I no longer had the time. Some came and took John out to lunch now and then to give me a few hours of respite, and a few hours of joy for John while he was in their company. Many of our friends sent monetary donations off and on for years that helped pay for John's therapy. We are truly grateful for everything everyone did, whether it is mentioned here or not. My memory has faded after twenty-five years of caregiving. I hope others that provided services not mentioned here will forgive me for my memory lapses.

After John's stroke, our lives, however, took a ninety degree turn and went in a totally different direction from the professional music business. The muse that we previously followed, which created our lifestyle, kept moving forward. I realized that our social paradigm had shifted, and that if we were to have any sort of social life, we would have to find different friends. We would have to rebuild our social lives and friendships by finding new friends that had more in common with our new lifestyle. This was a ponderous process and it took years to find and build the close relationships with new people that fit our new lives.

On loneliness and isolation

I read years ago, in a magazine or book I have long forgotten, about the isolation of people with handicaps. It is amazing how the Universe guided me to learn about this facet of people with handicaps before I knew I would be involved with someone with a severe handicap and one who uses a wheelchair outside of the home. Two items in what I read struck me most profoundly. One of them jolted me into personal action. The fact that most affected me when I read whatever it was I read, was that people with handicaps suffer from severe loneliness and isolation. They exist in a post ADA United States with the ability to be out in society, but for the most part, largely invisible and ignored.

The second item I read stated that since most people do not or cannot handle interacting with the person in a wheelchair, that that person literally avoids eye contact with those who are not handicapped. What happens is that they become invisible, like an ostrich with their head in the sand. The persons with handicaps adopt this behavior not only to protect others from having to make eye contact with them, but also to protect themselves from the constant pain of the awareness that they are invisible to the general public. It is just easier to not be reminded that they are invisible.

I decided to test the theory purported in what I read. As I walked on public streets, shopped in stores, malls, and everyplace I went, I made a conscious effort to make eye contact with people using wheelchairs. The numbers of them were astounding. Prior to this exercise I had never noticed how many of them there were. How many people using a wheelchair did you notice in your travels today? To my sad surprise, I discovered that it was all true! Most people in wheelchairs will not make eye contact with people whom they do not know. Even when I tried saying "hello", they avoided me. Oftentimes they exhibited shock at the fact that someone spoke to them. How lonely they must be. They are largely an invisible being in a world that either cannot or will not interact with them.

I wonder now how long it will take before their condition of being in a wheelchair is so normal, that they are no longer exiles from humanity. The world has made great strides in a positive direction for all of us, but the reality is that we are "not there yet". Most people using wheelchairs are still ignored, outside of their immediate family and friends, when they are out in public.

༺༻

My role of Caregiver has left me more than a little isolated. I have lost social skills along the way. I now spend most of my time alone, or with John, which is little more than being alone. I suffer as quietly as I can about this. I know that no one wants to hear me whine about my loneliness. I am not fun to be around either. I am boring and fearful. I am afraid I might slip and say something about my unhappiness and it is no secret that no one wants to be around someone who is unhappy. I have no doubt that people sense my fear and that becomes a catch-22. My fear compounds the fear of me in others which makes me more fearful. I sense their fear every moment.

I feel so alone, and so apart from my friends and the rest of the world.

I still have to "act" the part of being happy most of the time. Sometimes it comes out naturally. Most of the time I just get exhausted from the effort to appear happy. I do not want to alienate those around me. I wish I thought I was succeeding.

The energy it takes for me to pretend that I am happy when I am with my friends or in a public situation is mind-numbing and physically exhausting. It is no wonder I leave events early and simply retreat to the private sanctuary of my home to rest. I cannot keep up the façade. Even with my years as a performer, where I can "put on" any face, or as a teacher, where the boundary between teacher and student protected me from having to really interact with my students as people, I still tire from the energy level required to be social.

☙

There is a beautiful side to all of this. John and I changed. Our life path changed. We met and interacted with a host of new people. The new people we now meet see us as we are now. They did not know us before the stroke drew a line in the sand for us. It is easier for them to accept who we are.

John is luckier than I in this aspect. He is a naturally happy person and the stroke did not take that from him. For this I am extremely grateful. He lost far more than I did as a result of the stroke and he truly awakens each day, looking forward to being alive for that day.

I do know, each and every day, that I am lucky that I have so much awareness of my condition, of John's condition, and of how we appear to others. I am aware of how challenging it must be for those around us to be able to accept who we are now even though they did not know us in the "before" existence. My awareness helps me cope with an enormous amount of resistance from others. I feel that most others resist who we are, a couple with one person who has a handicap, not because they want to. I feel they resist us because they are not prepared to cope with the handicap and lack of social skills we convey. They resist because they are uncomfortable and do not know what to do. We are not the norm.

I truly do not judge them in any way for this. They are who they are, and are travelling their path in this life. Some people allow us "in" to their lives, if only for the occasional dinner out. Most others are not able only because their path has taken them to different lessons. I have no right to judge others. I am aware. There is a difference. Judging leaves me in a swirl of negative emotions. Awareness allows me compassion for them and for us. Compassion is a positive emotion and gives me hope. I know that my compassion is healing for me, for John, and for those around us. I hope that I will always appear to others as being compassionate. What a great gift that is!

Of course it may also be that my perception of their resistance is merely a reflection of my resistance to them. That however, is an entirely different and extremely lengthy discussion that is outside the parameters of my purpose at this point. I prefer to focus on the gifts and compassion. It brings me much more joy.

ଔ

On socializing and creating new friends

For several years, I volunteered with Habitat for Humanity. I did a variety of things with them, mostly relating to event planning, Homeowner's Association Law, and other Real Estate related committee work. This opportunity brought John and I into many social situations where we were routinely invited, encouraged, and accepted as a part of the group events. All of these events were extremely important to us socially as they brought us in contact with people who were not musicians. The socialization with these wonderful people taught us that there were indeed other people in the world with whom we could learn to feel comfortable outside of our social-box as musicians.

Another wonderful couple occasionally invites us to a day of "play" at Disneyland. They are musician friends that we have known since long before John's stroke. The feeling of being included and remembered for these events is monumental for us. It is a day of joy with our past "life" as musicians as we converse about gigs, music, and the music business while we wait in the lines for park attractions. In this particular venue, the park itself is extremely accessible for people with handicaps and we do not feel awkward at all. These days are great blessings for us as for that one day, we fit in. We are a part of the world of those having fun. Isolation disappears for a day.

> **Suggestions for Creating a New Social Life**
>
> Get out and volunteer with organizations that need you. Their gratitude for your help with their sense of purpose, their passion, brings you into their fold of friendship and social events.
>
> Stay in contact with past friends when it is appropriate and fun for all. You may have to make the effort to remain in contact with them as their lives have not changed, yours has.
>
> Most importantly, the Caregiver must make the effort to create events in your home and be involved in new areas outside of the home where there is the potential

> for friendship building. Do something different, find a new organization to join, get creative with your time and get out of the house, away from your duties as Caregiver. It is good for both of you. Plus, you never know what new friendships or social activities may appear as a result of your entrepreneurship in the world of friend-building.

On the most important lesson: forgiveness

The message of all of this is simple. For us, it is about forgiveness. The weight of carrying around resentment and anger at our friends for disappearing was lifted the moment we forgave our friends and forgave ourselves.

This forgiveness was a two-step process. First, we had to learn to forgive our friends for fading out of our lives. Our lives changed, not theirs. We were the ones who took the ninety degree turn in a different direction. In reality, we were and still are challenging to be around. Wheelchairs, accessibility, the lack of conversation on John's part, and other less important issues all became items that are uncomfortable for others to be around. We no longer fit into their "box" of social skills. Our skills changed, not theirs. It became our place to accept their discomfort and move into different social sets.

I also realized very quickly that not everyone is capable of dealing with people with handicaps. Not everyone has the same skill set. If they could not deal with it, then their discomfort became our discomfort. More importantly, I also know that many of our friends were so devastated by the loss of John as a friend, that their grief made it virtually impossible for them to see John in this condition. Our hearts go out to them. Our compassion towards them in their hours and years of grief has helped us forgive them without question.

Second, we had to forgive ourselves for judging our friends as "bad" for abandoning us. In reality, they did not abandon us at all. They are still overjoyed to see us when we take the time to venture into their musical lives and be present with them. We realized that we moved out of their lives. They did not move out of ours. We must make the effort to be present in their lives. Thus it was not our place to judge them at all. When we learned to forgive ourselves for our judgment of them, our pain burden was lifted.

Forgiveness is the greatest healer of all. Forgiveness lifts the weight of the burden off the shoulders of everyone involved. It is now easy to visit with our pre-stroke friends when we can, because our burden of resentment is no longer present for us. We have accepted the paradigm shift of our different social skills. We have found joy by forgiving our friends and ourselves.

Hearts Open to All

*When our hearts are open to all,
our caregiving is light and easy.*

Nancy Weckwerth

> *We give care to the grateful person*
> *who deeply appreciates our effort.*
> *We give care to the ungrateful curmudgeon*
> *who reviles us and resents us as intrusive.*
>
> *Since our actions need no reward,*
> *those who oppose us*
> *and those who welcome us*
> *are equally seen as friends.*

"The Caregiver's Tao Te Ching" by William and Nancy Martin

Chapter 10
Re-creating the Joy of Travelling

Life is a continual adventure that does not stop just because you are a Caregiver for a loved one. If you enjoy travelling, do it! You need the break away from the routine for your own self-care. Plus, you and your ward need to be away from each other for "vacations", too. I highly recommend time off for both of you. Recreation is called re-<u>create</u>-tion for a reason. It will help you come back to your duties refreshed, hopefully somewhat rested, excited to see your friend, and share what you have seen or done. What a wonderful opportunity to start a new line of conversation on a bunch of new topics for both of you!

I am providing solutions for travel under two different circumstances:

1. where the Caregiver travels and the Survivor is home alone
2. when Caregiver and Survivor are travelling away from home and exploring the world together

On Caregiver travel while leaving your Survivor at home

In my opinion, if the person for whom you care is stabilized enough to leave them at home alone while you travel, you are in a wonderful position on many levels. The first is that you get away. It is an opportunity for respite. The second is that it develops self-confidence on the part of the person that normally has you taking care of so many things for them. Third, it is an opportunity for your Survivor to learn new skills. Self-reliance is a huge step in their growth and healing.

I only suggest leaving them alone at home if they are truly able to care for themselves and have certain safety issues within their control. I cannot possibly know what criteria are important for every Caregiver and Survivor, and cannot be held liable for the decisions and choices you make.

What I considered as criteria for me to leave John at home alone after his stroke in 1991, were the following:

1. able to bathe and dress himself
2. able to get his food and warm it in the microwave
3. able to take care of our cats: feed, water, clean the litter
4. knows to turn off the stove or oven if used
5. keeps the doors locked—NEVER answers the front door

6. knows how to call for help if needed
7. knows to put trash in the trash bin
8. able to entertain himself
9. do his own laundry if needed
10. knows how to use the dishwasher

Hopefully this list will help you make your own choices about what your criteria are.

༄

When the Survivor is left at home alone, one of the big factors becomes loneliness. They have lost their main human contact while you are away. If they are aphasic from any kind of brain damage, this loneliness sometimes leads to a minor shut down of their abilities for their normal daily activities. They forget how to do things once they are out of their usual daily pattern.

When I was at home, if John filled the dishwasher himself, I usually found dishes on top of one another so that they would not get clean. I just restacked it before I turned it on. I decided that I would "let go" of the need for the dishwasher to be loaded correctly while I was travelling and deal with any issues of unclean items when I got back.

Other behavioral issues may surface, too. For example, whenever I travelled and left John alone for a few days, he would always break something in the house. One time I came back from three days away and John had broken the dishwasher. Part of his daily chores had always been to empty the dishwasher and put away the clean dishes. This was normally not a problem. He also knew how to fill the dishwasher, put detergent in it, and turn it on. In order to make sure that he got it on the correct cycles, I put duct tape over all of the knobs and cycles that he should NOT use. Then he would turn the starter knob to just the correct cycle.

When I returned from that one trip, there was a large hole in the inside top of the dishwasher. I am not exactly sure how he managed to break the dishwasher while I was away. John could not explain it to me, of course. I am not even sure he knew it had happened. My best guess is that he put a large knife or utensil of some kind in the top shelf. When he started to pull out the top shelf to unload it, the utensil dropped partially and caused the shelf to jamb. He could not figure out why the shelf would not come out so he just yanked on it until it rolled out of the dishwasher. He really is quite strong with his one good arm. My guess is that the utensil or the housing of the shelf ripped a hole in the dishwasher. Fortunately I was only away a couple of days and he did not use the dishwasher again. Otherwise we would have had copious amounts of water on the floor.

Almost $500.00 worth of new dishwasher later, John and I had a stern discussion about him paying attention to what he was doing. I taught him to bend over and look to see what was wrong. Most importantly, I tried to teach him to think before he acted. He never made that mistake again so I am assuming he either learned something, or just did not have an item fall through the top shelf again. This was the most expensive of his breakage events while I was away, but there was always something.

I actually wonder if that part of this behavior was in retaliation, subconsciously, for my leaving him alone. I cannot know if that is how his damaged brain works, but the trick for me was to let go of his potential motives, and simply deal with the clean up when I got home. This ability to let go of the details of the household chores allowed me to enjoy my travels. This is what created the respite for me. That is what created the joy.

ଓ

On leaving your Survivor alone

Whenever I travelled, I always made arrangements for my neighbor, Ellen, and after she died, her daughter, Kathryn, to stop in on a daily basis. They had keys to the house. They would check and see that the cats were all still alive and that the house was not full of water. Both Ellen and her daughter Kathryn, a registered nurse, had the kind heart and the skills to manage any issues. They also had my cell phone number so no matter where I travelled, they could reach me. Ellen would stop in whenever it was convenient for her. But Kathryn always stopped by when she got home from work. We were blessed with wonderful and caring neighbors.

Before I left I would type up a long list of instructions for all things in the house. This list included John's doctor's phone number and the phone number of our veterinarian. Of course it also included my complete itinerary with hotel phone numbers, locations, and airline flight information. I left John with emergency money in case he ran out of milk or cat food and arranged for neighbors to shop for him if needed. This shopping was really a backup plan. I stocked the pantry quite well before I left. These instructions were given to the neighbors and others who would be stopping by. In addition, copies of them were posted on the refrigerator door. John could read them there, too. The instructions on the refrigerator door were a comfort to John because he knew I had planned for every foreseeable circumstance that I could think of for him. He felt safe.

Our home telephone was completely programmed for one touch dialing for John. He could call me anytime he wanted. I worked with him to get him to understand the concept of "call me in emergencies only". Other than that, he was to call Ellen or Kathryn. I would try and call him every couple of days as a surprise for him.

Whenever I travelled, I filled the refrigerator and cupboards with John's favorite foods. John has only one arm so he cannot use a can opener. Thankfully most cans, including cat food cans, now have pull tabs on them to open them. John used his mouth to hold on to the pull tab and pull the can away from his face until it opened. This was a solution until his front tooth finally broke off from doing that. He no longer opens pull tabs. Like a typical six-year-old, John's favorite foods are junk food chips, cookies, and other such non-nourishing items. It is difficult enough to get anything green in him when I am home, but while away, I simply did not bother to provide anything from the vegetable or fruit food groups. I resigned myself to the concept that 2-4 days of only junk food would not permanently scar him. I wanted him to eat things he really liked as a treat so it would be fun for him while I was away.

Another solution for the food issue for us was the local "Meals on Wheels" service. We used that for a number of years. They normally came three times a week when I was working full time away from home. The volunteers who delivered them were amazing people who would follow instructions most of the time. These volunteers were told to come to the side door of the house to deliver the meals. I taught John that he was never, ever, to answer the front door of the house for safety reasons. When I travelled, I changed the meal delivery to five days a week. This provided not only food, but another human being for John to talk to each day. They also made sure John was OK in the mornings.

Since Kathryn or Ellen stopped by later in the day, there was someone coming into the house twice a day. I was comfortable with this. I just learned to trust that the Universe would protect him while I was away re-creating myself.

Another neighbor who watched over our house whether we were home or away, was Emilio. Emilio lived behind us. He worked for a local police department. I always let him know when I was going to be away. Knowing his eyes were on our house provided great comfort to me. If anyone knows how to spot something unusual, it is a cop. He always knew if a stranger was wandering in our yard or parking near our house. Another great neighbor with whom we were blessed!

We had two wonderful pet cats: J.S. Bach, and Marina Scriabin (better known as Bach and Marina). John was fully capable of doing "kitty litter" duty, feeding, and making sure they had water. When I got back, there was usually a mess on the floor next to the litter boxes as John's ability to sweep and clean spilled litter was non-existent. When I was not around, the cats were not finicky and ate anything John put in front of them. This always amazed me. For some reason they treated my feeding ritual quite differently and often attempted to "bury" the food I put down in front of them.

My last long trip away was a trip to Costa Rica for ten days to attend a Real Estate training seminar. In addition to all of the food and safety visits described above, I added another layer of assistance for John. I hired a dear friend to come by every two to three days and do the kitty litter with great intensity. She had a key so she could come in when it was convenient after work. If John was napping or practicing his trumpet, he would not necessarily hear a knock on the side door. Betsy was a colleague in my office. A more kind and wonderful human being probably does not exist on this planet. Betsy would stop in, take care of the kitty litter and chat with John for a while. Betsy also had instructions to get to the house as soon as possible in case of little natural California issues like earthquakes. She would know what to do and could leave work at the drop of a hat if necessary.

These visits by neighbors and delivery people provided a break in John's day and helped keep the loneliness away. With John's speech so limited, he no longer called his old friends. They have all faded away from regular interaction with him. I left numbers for his friends in case he really wanted to call them. But to my knowledge he never did. It is just too difficult for him to speak to them. He did call his mother while she was still alive, and his son whenever he wanted to do so. I had his son prepped with the information that I was away. John's son lives in Florida. It wasn't as if he could drop by to check on his dad. All of these outlets provided the antidote to loneliness.

Another part of the same antidote is John's own diligence regarding his daily schedule. He practiced his trumpet for a couple of hours, had lunch, napped, and then wrote music for a couple of hours. This is still his daily schedule. This non-variance of his routine helped keep him busy and productive while I was away. He has always been able to entertain himself and for this, I am extremely grateful. Most of the time, the visits I arranged from neighbors or friends were an interruption of his schedule. Too bad, John, you will be interrupted while I am away.

All of these solutions we used for leaving John at home while I was away, may or may not work for everyone. It is up to each Caregiver to find their own methods. I cannot be held liable for someone else's use of our methods because of all of the variables in each situation. In my opinion, each Caregiver's best judgment is the deciding factor for any methodology they may adopt.

ೞ

On travelling with your Survivor

I love to travel to places I have never been before. So does John. We decided we would do as much travelling as our situation allowed financially and physically. In the now twenty-five years since his stroke, we have taken many trips. They included two to Canada to visit his family. We made two trips to Minnesota to visit my relatives. We even took one to Florida for the marriage of his son. Our three biggest trips were seven days each to Maui and Kauai, in Hawaii, and Puerto Vallarta, Mexico. Other than these, we have had a few short two or three day trips around southern California just for a quick change of pace. We enjoyed all of them immensely from the adventure standpoint.

All these trips were when I was considerably younger. It became most apparent on the trip to Puerto Vallarta that our days of this type of travel were numbered. We discovered that most countries outside of the United States are not as accessible for people with disabilities as is the USA. In Puerto Vallarta, for example, if they even had a wheelchair ramp for stairways into hotels or restaurants, they created them by pouring and leveling concrete between the steps that were already in place. There appeared to be no standards there for the angle or length of the wheelchair ramp. Thus I was pushing a wheelchair up a ramp that was usually at a forty-five degree angle. The physical challenge of getting a 165 pound person plus wheelchair up a ramp of this angle cannot be minimized. Often times, these ramps connected only two steps and were so short that the back of the wheelchair would hit the ground at the bottom of a sidewalk ramp (as they intended it) and catch in the concrete, rock or dirt street. Most sidewalks in Puerto Vallarta do not have the ample curb cuts now required by law in the USA. That meant any site-seeing where there were sidewalks caused me to have to lift the front of the wheelchair up onto the sidewalk, and then lift him and the back of the chair onto the sidewalk. After seven days of this kind of lifting, my back began telling me that this was not acceptable behavior on my part.

Another challenge of Puerto Vallarta was that many of the streets on which we had to travel were unpaved, or paved with large river rocks. Pushing a wheelchair through dirt, gravel, or through river rock cobblestones is worse than pushing a wheelchair in grass. Simply crossing the street was a major ordeal. John could easily bounce right out of his chair if I was not extremely careful. The time factor of crossing these streets within the safe crossing lights can be a real challenge, too.

In the United States, the Americans with Disabilities Act was enacted in 1990. This legislation makes it possible to travel almost anywhere in the United States and know that there are accessible hotels, restaurants, and restrooms. Travel in State and National parks is easier because they will usually have a printed brochure of accessible areas of the parks. Most theme parks also have printed brochures and maps of areas that are the routes accessible for wheelchairs.

LESSON LEARNED

Travel only in countries that have standardized laws for ease of movement for people in wheelchairs or with other disabilities.

On surviving airports

Ah, the boisterous atmosphere and experience of airports: how lucky we are to have them. How fraught with ticklish issues for people with handicaps, in spite of the airport's best intentions!

We always travelled with John's personal wheelchair. When boarding a plane, I would push his wheelchair to the door of the plane. John could walk short distances so he would get out of his chair and walk down the aisle to his seat, using the seats themselves as his handrail/cane. Fortunately we were always able to pre-board to allow his slow process to his seat inconvenience as few other travelers as possible. Once he got out of his chair at the entrance to the plane itself, the staff would take his pre-checked wheelchair to the luggage compartment. It was always returned to us at the end of the flight for our use. We were first-on, and last-off with this routine.

Here is a charming and somewhat alarming tale of one of our travel adventures from Los Angeles, California, to Toronto, Canada. We left Los Angeles International (LAX) around 8:00 a.m. on a winter's day in late 2000. We were visiting John's Canadian mom prior to her moving to a Senior Care facility. After leaving LAX late, our flight stopped enroute for what was supposed to be a one and a half hour layover. Because of this short time, we checked his personal wheelchair straight through to Toronto and arranged for an airport wheelchair to meet us at the gate for our use during a quick dinner in the airport. Due to some nasty winter weather in our stopover city, our flight was delayed again by two and a half hours. What should have left around 7:30 p.m. did not leave until close to 10:00 p.m. We were trapped in the airport, moving around, waiting, eating, waiting, etc.

At the airport, the restaurant would not allow us to park an airport wheelchair anywhere near our dinner table. We had to leave it outside the restaurant in the terminal corridor. (Be advised, this was a violation of ADA law.) Thus, when I went to get it to load John after dinner and bring him to our gate, someone else had made off with our airport wheelchair. YIKES!!! I had to run all over the airport to negotiate another chair for us to make our flight.

> **LESSONS LEARNED**
>
> Always have your own chair brought to the gate for use in the airport. Even if you have to leave it outside a restaurant, most people in an airport would not make off with a private chair. Someone had assumed the airport chair had been abandoned and taken it for someone else's use.
>
> Take advantage of airport services and ask for help within the airport.

༄

The Toronto Adventure

By the time we landed in Toronto, it was after 1:00 a.m. the next day and we were hours late. We had arranged for a rental car at the Toronto airport for us to drive to his mother's apartment. When we landed in Toronto, I had now been moving John and our luggage all by myself, for over seventeen hours. We learned we had to take a shuttle bus from our terminal to the rental car booths in another terminal. That meant I moved all luggage into the shuttle bus, moved John into the bus, then lifted his chair into the storage area of the bus. That shuttle took us to the other terminal near the rental car booths. We then had to disembark from the shuttle bus. The next task was to remove all luggage, get John out of the shuttle, lift the wheelchair down, load John into his wheelchair, and move both a tired John and our luggage into the terminal. We found the rental car booths only to discover a sign that said: "Closed at midnight. Take the shuttle bus to the satellite rental car area to get your cars after midnight." Therefore I had to transport our little caravan to a different shuttle area and wait for the shuttle bus to take us to the satellite rental car buildings. They were a mile or more from the main airport. Then I loaded John, luggage, and wheelchair into yet another shuttle bus. When we arrived at the satellite rental car buildings, it was 2:45 a.m. and they closed all of the satellite buildings at 3:00 a.m. I got to unload John, luggage and chair out of the bus and enter the satellite building. There was one other couple collecting their car when we arrived. By the time we got to the desk to get our car, it was 2:55 a.m. and there was literally only one car left in the rental car lot. It was now over eighteen hours of moving luggage, wheelchair, and John. Next I had to load all of our respective caravan components into a rental car and drive to his mother's apartment. This was about a forty-five minute drive.

We arrived at his mother's apartment building about 4:00 a.m. I unloaded John in bitter cold weather, ice, and wind, close to the door of her security locked building. Then I drove almost a block away to park in the guest parking and walked back to the security door. It took maybe fifteen to twenty minutes to wake his mother and get her to buzz us in the door. Once in the door, I moved luggage, John in his wheelchair and me, (thoroughly exhausted) into the door, up an elevator and into her apartment. Ninety-year-old sweetheart that she was, she was of course delighted to see us. After a quick hello, the moving of all luggage, John, and myself into a small bedroom, I finally collapsed in bed just before 5:00 a.m.

Tired yet? I am exhausted just writing it all down!

A few hours later at 7:30 a.m., his dear mother knocked on our bedroom door and said, "Good morning, breakfast is ready!" It never occurred to this sweet old woman that we had been travelling for almost twenty-four hours with just over two hours of sleep! I begged for a couple more hours. She gracefully complied. But she did so without really understanding the situation.

I eventually got up around 9:00 a.m. Then I bathed John in a strange bathroom without the assistance of a shower seat. He was always terrified when bathing in a different bathroom because his "habitual" patterns of how he did it were changed. Change was and still is difficult for John. We ate a quick breakfast. Then I was informed that John's aunt Marjorie and their dear friend, Dorothy, were arriving by taxi. Since we had a rental car, they wanted to take us to a museum and out to lunch around 11:00 a.m. These three gals, all now deceased, were the three most charming and kind women in the world. None of them drove. The public transportation and taxi-cabs in Toronto are marvelous. For them, the treat of a car with driver was a major event. They could not wait to be ferried around Toronto and enjoy our company. They were SO excited to see us.

Now here is the rub—all three of them needed assistance to get in and out of a car, due to their advanced age. With four people needing assistance, the "assistant" had to be me! Thus we began our day of events in Toronto. Each stop required the requisite unload and load of four people. I remained as cheerful as possible. However my total exhaustion was beginning to make cheer almost impossible. I do recall making a couple of what I now consider caustic comments about something over lunch. I have often felt guilty about those comments.

LESSONS LEARNED

Other people are not aware of the difficulty of moving a person in a wheelchair and luggage around their own stomping grounds, let alone travelling almost three thousand miles by plane, moving luggage, and your Survivor. If family members and friends do not deal with wheelchairs and people with handicaps daily, they cannot be expected to understand the extreme fatigue involved for the Caregiver.

It requires that the Caregiver educate, as gracefully as possible, friends and family members to prepare them for your visit.

There is no reason to judge those who do not understand, it is just outside of their personal "box" of experience. It is up to you, the Caregiver, to maintain a sense of humor and make the best of the situation. After all, the Caregiver gets to be of service, which is a gift given to you by the Universe because you, as Caregiver, are strong enough to do it. Be grateful that the Universe has chosen you to be a Caregiver. It is a very special gift.

I hope you will learn from this story, and accept the following travel hints on making it easier on both Caregiver and Survivor.

Suggests for Travelling with a Person in a Wheelchair

Book direct flights as often as possible. A touch-down is no big deal as long as you do not have to change planes.

Keep your personal wheelchair with you if have to deplane and amuse yourself in an airport for a few hours.

Arrange for transportation at both ends of the trip that does not involve you getting a rental car late at night.

You cannot possibly foresee the events that could occur when travelling. Flights get delayed, luggage gets lost, and wheelchairs walk away of their own accord.

Although there are porters and others in an airport to assist with luggage, know that they do not get you on and off shuttle buses, in or out of taxis, or in and out of your rental cars at your destination locales. The best laid plans cannot guarantee this process flows according to the plan.

Hire a travel companion whose job it is to move luggage and the person using a wheelchair for you. It is not possible to enjoy a trip or "vacation" under the above circumstances as related. It is not restful or recreational.

Others do not understand this. Send love and light to those others and know that their life-experience may not include having been a Caregiver.

When booking hotels, request rooms that are ADA compliant. Sometimes this is an issue. The most important thing is accessibility. If there are no elevators and you have a second floor room with a person in a wheelchair, no amount of handrails in the bathroom solve your biggest challenge: getting them TO the room. Not all hotels have wheelchair accessible rooms. I have also experienced the line "by availability only", which means, you can get an accessible room ONLY if they are not already taken. This is not a reservation; this is a ploy to get you to book the hotel without knowing what amenities will be available for you. Find another hotel that will RESERVE an accessible room. I recently experienced a situation where the rooms were "availability only" and when we arrived at the hotel, all the available accessible rooms were on the main floor at TWICE the price of the room I had booked online. We were sitting ducks for an upcharge and they were laughing behind our backs.

Most importantly, forgive yourself for any hostile, angry or caustic remarks that arise as a result of your extreme fatigue. Self-forgiveness is one of the greatest blessings that we can accept as Caregivers. No one is perfect. (But in my humble opinion, I think Caregivers are closer than most.) We are viewed by others as saints only as far as their own experience can reveal to them. They cannot possibly know the depth of your care or of your fatigue. Be at peace. Know that you were chosen for this opportunity to care for others. You were chosen because the Universe knows you are strong. It knows you are a loving person. It knows you can forgive yourself for any self-judgments of possible shortcomings. The Universe trusts you or you would not have been given this special joy.

Experience is a great teacher. I no longer take long trips away from John. I only travel with him on very well organized short trips. His and my advancing years have decreed that experiencing these adventures must be weighed very carefully. Therefore, take the opportunities to travel while you are young, or at least very young at heart. Life is way too short to miss these adventures. Your life does not stop when catastrophic illness invites itself into your life. The world is an amazing and wonderful place. See it, experience it. No matter what happens to you that makes you tired or may discourage you, remember that nothing can equal the joy of experiencing new cultures, food, scenery, or events. The experiences themselves will rejuvenate you!

All of the details that I described above are just that, details. Never let the details get in the way of the adventure. Keeping the fact that challenges are merely details is your salvation and allows both of you to experience life. Life is always an adventure, whether it be staying at home or getting out on the open road. Cherish and accept the opportunity for those adventures. Choose wisely, be flexible, travel light, and always enjoy. Your lives will be richer for having embraced the opportunity. This richness brings with it a sense of accomplishment. It also gives priceless memories of that adventure that can only be created by the adventure itself.

When studying the Tao excerpt quoted below, I am reminded that simply letting go of all of the potential traumas involved with travel is the solution to successful travel experiences. I have also learned from those past experiences, how to make travel do-able and very rewarding for John and me. I no longer keep a mental list of things that went wrong. Instead I focus on all of the things that have gone right. I have learned to do what is required to make the trip enjoyable.

I do not exist with expectations of rewards from being John's Caregiver either. Expectations frequently lead to disappointments. With no expectations, I simply accept the joy and the wonder of the travel experiences as they arrive. Each moment of joy is its own reward.

Nothing Needed in Return

If we keep a tally sheet,
balancing effort against reward,
our work will surely breed resentment.

*When circumstances are difficult,
we do whatever is necessary.
Neither resentment nor blame arise
because nothing is needed in return.*

*Our reward is independent
of the changes in external events.
It resides within our nature
and is always with us.*

"The Caregiver's Tao Te Ching" by William and Nancy Martin

Chapter 11

The Pro-Active Caregiver: Patient Advocacy

As in all aspects of life, there are different levels of skills involved relative to the professionals with whom we all work. All of us have seen the negative news reports regarding teaching professionals, clergy, or day care situations, to mention a few. Most professionals are wonderful, caring, talented, and worthy of your trust and respect. Some are not so wonderful or caring, certainly not talented, and definitely not worthy of your trust and respect.

It is no different in the medical profession at any level. Just because an individual has "Doctor" before his or her name, or they have a lot of diplomas on the wall, does not make that person good at what he or she does. It means they have met a **minimum** set of standards or qualifications to do their job. No one knows what grades that person got on their medical exams. We all know grades in themselves are not the only indicator of skill, knowledge, or wisdom. Grades do tell you about the diligence of those who earned them. They do reveal whether they cared enough to learn the material that they were expected to learn. Any medical school graduate could have been at the top of their class or, they could have been the one who barely graduated. It is the same thing for airplane pilots. Our society tends to deify the medical profession in that we automatically accept that what they say or do is "the best way, or the only way" to do something. Seriously, there is more than one way to do almost anything.

This carries over into the other areas of medical and disciplinary services, too. Therapists, social workers, hospital personnel in all areas, whether they are medical staff, administrative staff, support staff, or officialdom of any kind, must be subject to your scrutiny at all times. A lofty position, fancy letters after their name on their door, or scrubs as a uniform does not guarantee that anyone is truly expert at their job.

I wish that life was perfect. I wish that everyone with whom we come into contact regarding the care of our loved ones was honest, bright, caring, and extremely good at what they do. I want to believe that most are.

Having said this, here is the most important caveat of this entire story. **One must be an active and present advocate on site at all times regarding the care of your loved one.** What happens when you are not looking can be nightmarish. I cannot stress this enough.

Here is a hypothetical example of what could occur in any facility: A young hospital assistant (job title unknown) pushes a woman in a wheelchair into an elevator in a well-respected hospital. This particular wheelchair is one where the woman's legs are kept straight out in front of her. This woman is incapable of moving herself at all. For some reason, the assistant carelessly bounces the wheels of the chair on the edge of the elevator. As a result, the woman screams and falls half way out of her chair. The assistant quickly hustles the woman back into the chair, gets in the elevator and speeds away. In this type of hypothetical situation, I can only wonder, where is the family for this poor woman? Why are they not present? Why are they not being an advocate for her?

I am ashamed to admit that my own issues with John during similar moments were so pressing that I would not have been able to take the time to report similar events that I may have witnessed to hospital administration. I only know that I was so emotionally drained from my personal ordeal that it would not have even occurred to me to do so.

Here is the danger. The emotional and physical exhaustion of caring for someone in a catastrophic illness situation takes you, the Caregiver, out of your normal ability to discern, question, observe, or take action. Sometimes it even prevents you from caring about anything outside your sphere of reference and your personal responsibilities.

What if it was your loved one who fell out of the chair? Would you not want someone who witnessed it to report that incident on behalf of your loved one? Do not count on it, ever. The only one who will be there for your loved one is YOU. It is your responsibility. You are the advocate for the patient!

Had I been in this situation, I would probably feel guilty that I was not able to speak to someone about witnessing this dangerous mistreatment of a patient. I now know I must forgive myself for any guilt. I most likely would have been doing everything that I could do at that moment. It would have been beyond my capability to add another layer of advocacy for someone I did not know.

CR

The being "hospitalized" situation is truly a nightmare for your loved one, too. If they are aphasic, as John was, they feel pain, but cannot necessarily express that they do. They cannot tell you that something happened to them. They cannot tell you the food they are being fed is abysmal, cold, or not there at all. They cannot tell you their clothes hurt or that their sheets are wet. They cannot express alarm that no one takes them to the bathroom, that they are not being bathed or any other of a million "care" situations that we just assume are taken care of in a professional manner. Just because these things *should* be taken care of, does not mean they are.

It is up to you to take charge of the situation because you know your family member. You know what they like, how they feel, how they react. Most importantly, you know who they are. You must observe not only the medical issues, but the personal care issues for the comfort of your ward.

ଔ

The Skilled Nursing Facility Saga

Here is another hypothetical example of why you need to be present with your loved one as much as possible. Be forewarned, this is very graphic.

At the facility where your loved one is staying, there may only be a limited number of restrooms per resident. When the caregiver arrives to assist their loved one with his or her toilet needs, the caregiver may frequently walk into the bathroom to be assaulted with the foul smell of walls, toilet, and toilet seat covered in nearly dried excrement. This may be a result of one of the other resident's difficulties. It is unfortunate, and in my mind unacceptable, that it is NOT cleaned up for quite some time. The caregiver's loved one may be forced to wait while the caregiver requests that the management staff cleans the bathroom. It may be likely that the staff will not rush to assist with the cleaning so caregiver and the loved one will have to find another bathroom in the facility. This type of hypothetical situation is completely intolerable and filthy.

Sadly, the staff simply may not do their duty of taking care of patients with the problem nor of cleaning the room. If the Caregiver was not there, the loved one could be left alone with no useable bathroom available for him or her within reach.

In my opinion, basic human dignity may not be the priority of the staff.

Solutions for the family and Caregiver(s)

The solution to such hypothetical examples is to be at the hospitals, and at the SNFs, as often as possible. Be an advocate constantly. Check the cleanliness of the rooms and bathrooms.

Observe how staff members treat other patients with regard to safety issues. If you see mistreatment of anyone, know that it could happen to your loved one, too. Be alert and constantly observe what is happening around you.

Share this duty with other family members or friends. It is in the moment that you leave that your wards are the most vulnerable, especially if they are paralyzed or unable to speak for themselves. Friends and family can assist with the observation aspect.

Be an educated consumer and ask questions. Use your best judgment as to what should be happening at this facility. It is much easier for you to ask questions about your patient if you are more aware of how they should be treated.

Always research potential treatments on the Internet. This will help you learn what your goals can be for the future of your loved one. You will learn what a facility can do for you, and if it cannot do what you need, you can research other facilities that will serve you better.

If there would have been any issues at the SNF, I would have gone directly to someone in administration and introduced myself. I would have told them what was occurring overnight in the bathrooms and requested their help. My advice is to get to know the administrators. They are really the *only ones* with the clout to institute real change.

CR

During the first year of his rehabilitation, John had an additional insurance policy that kicked in from the musicians' union. This happens with artists because a certain amount of qualifying work must be paid on a union job in each quarter of the year. Once that qualifying threshold is reached, health insurance kicks in several months later. That insurance is then in place for three to six months, depending upon your specific policy and qualification amounts. As a freelancer, without permanent employment, musicians and other performers are particularly vulnerable to the on-again, off-again insurance policy. In John's case, he was eligible for a set number of speech therapy sessions and about three months of Occupational Therapy, (OT) and Physical Therapy (PT) in a different HMO.

We decided that since this insurance was available, we may as well use it for therapy. We enrolled in Occupational, Physical, and Speech Therapy. These appointments were on top of the already twelve to fifteen appointments a week that John was receiving privately after he had been released from the SNF. The enrollment period started and John had his six months of insurance eligibility. The insurance time period eligibility did not match the therapy amounts of eligibility. Here is the additional rub—the therapy department was booked solid for two months and there was no room for John to come in for therapy. The insurance eligibility clock continued to tick. The speech department was also booked solid and John waited ninety days for appointments. As I recall, John was eligible for five weeks of speech therapy only, at one or two appointments a week.

The typical physical and occupational therapy appointment after we brought John into the facility followed what I believed to be a pattern. John would spend twenty minutes with a therapist, and they would work with him. It is my opinion that the therapy providers would merely shuffle patients from one vacant area of the facility to another vacant area without any observable plan for recovery.

These therapy rooms were filled with other people in need of therapy and attention. They were a bee-hive of activity. As I watched what was going on for the first six weeks of John's therapy, it is my opinion that it was not proceeding with any "plan" for his development. They would give him a task to do, walk away, and return later to see if he was still doing it. To my knowledge, there was no written "plan" for his therapy. The tasks seemed to me to be random, haphazard, and therefore, they were not about skill building. In both occupational and physical therapy, he met with a different therapist for each session. Wow! I was in shock. Although some therapy is better than none, I felt that John made absolutely no progress as a result of therapy during this time. If there was any record keeping on the part of the therapists, I never saw it.

Since I had been observing the therapy process and working with the therapists in other facilities, I knew that the therapy in this facility was not what John needed.

In my opinion, the speech therapy at this facility was even worse than the physical and occupational therapy. John was eligible for five weeks of speech therapy. By this time, a year into his stroke, he was already speaking a few words based upon the success of his private therapy. However, this therapist continued to administer "tests" to find out what John could and could not do for four weeks. At the end of her "testing" period, he had only one actual therapy session with her. I felt this was an example of a supposedly competent therapist simply punching a clock at work without doing any real "work". Again, this is only my opinion.

This entire experience exemplified, for me, our insurance dollars at work. I felt it was a joke. After some computation of the gas and time involved for the one hour drive each way to this institution, and the total lack of progress, we decided not to finish out the last couple of weeks of OT and PT. We had better ways to spend our time. We chose to spend our time working on our own or scheduling private therapists. I observed John make more progress as a result.

This is a prime example of how the Caregiver must be an advocate for the patient. In this instance, John was not mentally capable of making a judgment or decisions about whether or not any of this therapy was valid or helping him. He could not give any feedback. As a Caregiver, it was my job to evaluate the progress and efficacy of the treatments he was receiving, then, as it is now. Had I not been observing his therapy for the past six to eight months already, I would not have known that what they were doing was not helping. It was only because I had been active in his therapy all along, that I had gained the wisdom and awareness of what worked and what was wasting our time.

Solutions for the Caregiver

Observe all therapy and treatments when possible. It gives you as Caregiver a frame of reference for what progress is occurring and where there is no progress.

Be an active advocate of what is happening relative to all of the therapy modalities. Observe methodology, watch for record keeping, and ask about the "plan" for this patient.

Watch for supervisory personnel. If the professionals are not doing any of the above, or will not discuss it with you, move on. They are wasting your time and money. It is your job to educate yourself on what should be happening in therapy sessions and to make sure it is happening.

Educate yourself: use the Internet for learning about therapy in addition to your own observation. Talk to other patients; find out which therapy institutions have the best reputations for success. The best institutions cost money and if they are not covered by your insurance policy, negotiate private paid treatments with their staff. A small amount of therapy with a great therapist pays off in infinite ways.

Here is the best tactic for the Caregiver–LEARN what the therapist does and do it at home with your loved one.

> If you think you cannot, think again, it is your duty to bring your loved one to the best quality of life they can have. Here is why—their quality of life becomes YOUR quality of life.
>
> As a Caregiver, you cannot simply drop off the patient and go shopping. You must actively participate in the process and monitor the safety and progress of the therapy. Be the advocate that insures progress towards a successful recovery and the highest quality of life possible for your loved one. It will help you in the long run to observe and learn everything you can from these therapy sessions.

ෙන

Yet another arena where advocacy is critical is in the private medical offices or clinics where your loved one is being treated long after the hospital and therapy treatments have ended. It has taken years of mistakes I made as a Caregiver to seek out and use the doctors that are the best for John now.

Here is an example. John was seeing what we felt was a wonderful optometrist who was also an ophthalmologist, specializing in diseases of the eyes. We both saw this ophthalmologist for over fifteen years. John was diagnosed with glaucoma and was doing what we were told was the standard treatment for glaucoma. This standard treatment involves eye-drops daily to prevent further damage to the optic nerve. We were told eventually surgery could be performed, on a one-time-only basis to correct the problem. When the effects of that surgery wore off, there was nothing more that could be done and the patient would often go blind. Therefore the standard treatment is to keep the patient on the eye-drops as long as possible before this surgery is performed. The intention is to keep the patient "seeing" as long as possible.

As is typical, the eye-drop medications eventually lose their ability to be effective so the ophthalmologist changes to different drugs. When John got to this point the first time, and his eye pressures were rising, we changed medications. This next set of medications worked well for a number of years.

Then the second medications also lost their ability to keep his pressures down so we changed medications again. This time, John had a horrible allergic reaction to the medication and after two to three days, I called the ophthalmologist and we decided to stop that medication and try another type. I picked up the next bottle of eye drops and we proceeded to try them. John's eyes turned red, hot, and his lids started swelling within two hours. I stopped them immediately and called the ophthalmologist. We went in to the office, and asked if there was anything else we could do. In my opinion, the only reply was that there was no other option.

I felt appalled and disappointed at what I believed to be a total lack of empathy for John's issue.

When I arrived home after leaving that ophthalmologist's office, I immediately got on the Internet to search for additional glaucoma resources. I tried "glaucoma studies" as a Google Search term and located a study being done at the Doheny Eye Institute in the Los Angeles area. After few minutes of further research, I found that the Doheny had a branch office about fifteen minutes from where we lived. I booked an appointment online for two days later with a Glaucoma Research Specialist. All this took me thirty minutes at most.

Upon meeting John's new doctor at the Doheny Branch Office, we learned that some of the modalities we had learned about from the previous ophthalmologist were no longer state of the art. Laser surgery can now be performed over and over again to keep the eye pressures down. There are additional treatments that can be done to prevent blindness.

Medical science is amazing! It keeps marching forward giving hope where there was no hope previously. For that fact, we are both very grateful.

> **LESSONS LEARNED**
>
> There is no going back in time. All I can do now is forgive myself for making an unknown error and make sure that John has the best care possible, NOW. I have learned to let go of any anger that immediately occurs because anger does not serve me. Moving forward serves me, and it serves John.
>
> If you are unsure of, or believe that the treatment received by any doctor is less than treatments that are available, get a second opinion and/or CHANGE DOCTORS. This is advocacy from a different perspective. You are managing care in a non-acute situation where you have much more control.
>
> In general, if the doctors are not "there for you" or doing what you ask, change doctors. If they are not responding to questions or calls, change doctors. You cannot afford to "not be helped" when you ask for it. You have too many things to do. After all, you are hiring the doctor. You are their employer. They work for you, not the other way around.

Because I learned these lessons, I now change doctors or facilities much quicker before my frustration level builds. If the situation is not serving John medically, or assisting with making my life as Caregiver less problematic, I advocate for change quicker. My analysis skills have grown.

Finally, be at peace. Everyone has the right to make the decisions one needs to make and whatever decision one makes is the absolute right decision for each moment. All decisions can only be based upon the information and knowledge one has at that moment. If it turns out it was a bad decision, make another decision. After all, a decision is only a group of words created by thoughts in the brain. Thoughts can be changed. Maintain flexibility in all areas of life. Like a palm tree that bends in a hurricane, one's strength lies in the ability to bend so one does not break.

CR

It takes a monumental amount of personal stamina to supervise the care of your loved one. It also takes wisdom, clarity, courage, and most importantly, love, at all times and in all things. Staying within the realm of love-based emotions relieves one's burden and lowers stress. With less stress, one is able to make better decisions. Better decisions equal a higher quality of life for both the Caregiver and the Survivor. Everyone wins.

The Joy in Caregiving comes from having solved all of the problems. One's skill at providing the highest quality of life, not only for the Survivor, but also for oneself, transcends the time required to learn the lessons. Self-satisfaction occurs naturally. At this point, caregiving is the culmination of personal growth on the part of the Caregiver. When the burden is released, peace and joy are what remains. One can look at life, and honestly know that one has done the best possible job at every moment, in every day. What a wonderful awareness!

Yin and Yang

*The energies of yin and yang combine
to hold the universe together,
but we dearly want to cling to one
and have the other go away.*

*We didn't want this to happen,
but it has.
We want to know what will happen tomorrow,
but we can't.
We can only stand here at the center
and watch and breathe.
We feel alone and helpless,
but we're not.
Life weaves itself around us,
making us a part of all that is.*

"The Caregiver's Tao Te Ching" by William and Nancy Martin

Chapter 12
Moving through Mourning

Catastrophic illness draws a line in the sand–the life and relationships before the event, and the life and relationships after the event. They are forever different. The ability to accept and move through the change is the challenge that faces the person affected with the illness and the family supporting and caring for them. This movement toward change is a two stage process. First, everyone involved must mourn the end of the lifestyle and relationships before the event. Second, everyone must move forward to "the now" and carve out a new concept of one's life and relationships after the event.

I am not an expert in psychology, psychiatry, nor am I a grief counselor. However, I can research topics I wish to know about as well as anyone else can. Regarding mourning, I learned that the Kübler Ross Model of Mourning identifies five stages of mourning. This model is only one standard accepted by the medical field for use in treatment of critically and terminally ill patients. Although reasonably well known, it is not totally supported by documented clinical research. Other researchers refute the model. My purpose is not to debate its viability or the lack of it. Please see the Internet link in Appendix III to learn about Kübler Ross Model and other clinical models on grief and mourning.

I will discuss how John and I processed our own path of mourning using some of the terms of the Kübler Ross Model of Mourning. However, mourning is an individual process. Each person goes through their own process. Some of the emotions of the Kübler Ross model were processed by John and I individually, but not all of them since his stroke in 1991. Hopefully, learning how we processed the emotional curves will help others move through mourning and come out the other side, as we have–thriving in our new life.

I will describe the emotions the Kübler Ross Model identifies first. Then I will describe John's mourning process as I observed it. Next, I will describe the emotional path I followed. Finally, I will describe some emotions that we processed together.

There are five main emotional stages of mourning in the Kübler Ross Model: denial, anger, bargaining, depression and acceptance. Kübler Ross further emphasizes that not everyone will go through all stages and some individuals may go through additional emotional states. Remember, it is a tool, not a rule for each individual and their own process of mourning.

Briefly, *denial* is the emotional stage where we refuse to accept the facts of what has happened. *Anger* is truly the rage we feel when we realize that a profound change has occurred and we are not happy that we have to change and live differently. *Bargaining* is when we attempt to change an outcome by offering something in exchange for an unwanted outcome. *Depression* is the sadness that results as part of the beginnings of acceptance of the event. *Acceptance* is when someone has come to terms with the event and the changes that occur. *Acceptance* is really the paradigm shift that I described in an earlier chapter. In the case of life changing events, *acceptance* is the step into "the now" and it indicates a willingness to adapt to the new circumstance of life. This last step is the goal.

༄

John's journey through mourning

One of the things that I am most grateful for in this entire process is that the stroke took enough of John's brain that I believe he was and is not aware, totally, of how much he really lost in some areas of his life. I believe this from having been a part of his recovery and seeing the progress he has made. I know this from knowing him so well that I know his intentions and thoughts as a person and as a musician. This type of "knowing" is the greatest blessing of all. It has allowed us to trust one another as we have coped with his paralysis and inability to communicate with normal language skills.

When the stroke occurred on February 12, 1991, John became completely paralyzed on his right side and he lost his speech. He was expressive aphasic. This means he understood most of what was said to him, but he was unable to speak back, follow directions, or complete any of his Activities of Daily Living or ADLs. He was instantly transformed into a total invalid, dependent upon others for eating, bathing, and dressing. He was unable to hold a trumpet to play music. He was unable to write music at all. The stroke wiped out half of his body, his speech, his skills, his career as a musician, and his ability to make a living for us. I know that initially he completely gave up and decided that he may as well die. He felt he had nothing left. He had a lot to mourn.

I recently asked him if he was afraid when he woke up and realized what had happened to him. He told me "No, Nancy Weckwerth". I next asked if it was because I was "present", or did he "trust" me. He got very excited when I mentioned "trust". That is what did it for him. His trust in me pulled him out of fear and denial and into believing that together, we could do this. He trusted me implicitly, to help him recover. I am honored that he trusted me so much. He also trusted our ability, working together as a team, to take care of his needs. These items of trust are what made the difference for him and for me as Caregiver. Together we were able to turn this event into a totally new purpose for life. John has always been a resilient person and this event was certainly no exception. At first there were so many unknowns that we just took each event as it came and lived in "the now". He simply brushed aside all anger and moved forward.

I also believe that the stroke took away a lot of his capacity for anger. He does get angry now and then. However, it is always in frustration with his inability to communicate verbally. Surprisingly, John does not get angry about his lack of physical mobility. I believe that his acceptance of this lack of physical mobility is rooted in two things. First he saw himself as a totally un-athletic person as a child. The skill of athletic-like physical movement was never foremost in his sense of self. Second, his sense of purpose was totally wrapped up in being a musician and artist. Since he still sees himself as a musician and artist, he believes that was not compromised. Thus he really did not see a reason to be angry. He accepted his situation and was cognizant enough to "go on regardless" (which is one of his favorite sayings).

Moving forward for John meant that he had to play his trumpet again. John is one of those people who knew from childhood that the only thing he ever wanted to do was play the trumpet and write music. All he really cared about before the stroke and all he cares about since the stroke are those two things. This is actually what made him truly great as a musician and composer. He was and is the consummate artist. He really had not lost his musical talent, he was just re-acquainting his brain with his old self by finding skills that were temporarily lost. He worked hard and studied the beginning music reading books. He whipped through them like lightning in a stormy sky. He was quickly on track to acceptance of his supposed loss, because as far as he knew he had not lost it. He believed in himself. His acceptance is all that is important. He made the paradigm shift to his new life. How grateful we both are for this!

By the fourth or fifth year of practicing his trumpet daily, John could now actually perform on a music gig. We are grateful that he had the opportunity to perform in a church every Sunday. It gave him the sense of being a part of his previous career. The church paid him a small salary each week. He felt "professional" again. He worked every Sunday at this church for over two years. He finally tired of it because it was as he said "the same thing" over and over. He got bored.

I found a few other venues for him to rehearse with groups but they did not work out. Although he still has his same beautiful sound and accurate pitch while playing his trumpet, he has lost, unbeknownst to him, the ability to play in time with the other players. Without getting into extremely technical aspects of music performance, John cannot read the note values and perform them relative to the "beat" of the music. So he marches to a different drummer. If he hears it, he can follow along. But he is following. He is no longer the leader or principal trumpet player that he was. I am eternally grateful that he still believes he is. He accepts who he is as a musician and artist now. It fulfills him.

※

I, however, am not as easily soothed. Writing about this has reopened a gaping wound. I am weeping inconsolably as I write for what the world has lost for the past twenty five years in this man's performance and compositional skills.

I remember thinking that it has now been five years since the stroke and I still cannot listen to any music at all. I'm emotionally unable to cope with my pain. I've turned off the radio, ignored our collection of compact discs, and shut down the music in my head. This avoidance of hearing music at all is helping me cope with the loss of my career.

I'm literally numb, emotionally. I've stopped writing music. I'm also too busy taking care of John to really be aware that the ashes of my career are blowing away. All of this is really denial of what occurred in our lives. My grief is so intense that I'm becoming a caregiving automaton.

I still ache to be on stage again, competently playing my horn within a large ensemble where the sound waves vibrate through every cell of my body as I play. Competence is really the issue. There are not enough hours in my Caregiver's day to add practicing the mere four to six hours daily that it requires to perform on my instrument at the level of a professional brass player.

○○

My own journey through mourning

As John's Caregiver, my goal for him has always been to give him the highest quality of life possible. I carry no guilt within myself relative to his quality of life. I achieved my goal for him. My own movement through mourning has followed many more of the emotions mentioned in the Kübler Ross Model of Mourning than John's did.

I distinctly remember sitting underneath his hospital bed on day two after the stroke in shock and denial of what had occurred. The doctor had just told me it would be at least two years before he would work again, *if* he was able to work. My entire world collapsed. It was no less catastrophic for me than watching the twin towers fall ten years later in 2001. I really knew nothing about strokes at the time. I believed everything was just temporary. Little did I know that the rest of our lives would be devoted to healing, rehabilitation and thriving in an entirely new world. This was a world that was unknown to both of us.

○○

About six months after the stroke, I recall pushing John in his wheelchair from the local library, back to my job at the retail store. I was enraged. I did not want to spend the rest of my life pushing a wheelchair. It is demanding work. The person being pushed is not aware of the difficulty of lifting them up a curb or of avoiding sidewalk bumps. There is the eternal folding of the chair, putting it in or getting it out of the trunk of the car. My body ached then as it does now. I was angry a lot at this time. This was the anger of mourning for me. Well, it was one iteration of the anger. It was the first one that occurred where I was aware that I was really angry over all of this. The time up until this point had been solely of putting out the fires of acute care and change. My emotions were bouncing like a runaway beach ball.

I rarely allow myself the luxury of real anger. From childhood, I have suffered from migraine headaches. I learned long ago that any allowance of anger triggers a migraine headache for me. My methodology is to quickly let go of the anger, since it is really counterproductive on many levels. I certainly would prefer to avoid a migraine. Letting go is a great tool. Since I was aware of my very real anger in having to care for John, I decided quickly to let it go. It does not serve me to remain angry. Feel it, be aware that you feel it, and let it go. This formula means no forty-eight to seventy-two hour headaches. This lesson was learned many years ago. I am grateful

I was able to recall the lesson and use it regarding my anger over John's condition.

※

Depression has been a daily visitor in my life for many years—long before the stroke. It runs in my family. Heredity compounded with caregiving for someone with catastrophic illness is a working formula for depression. Caregiver exhaustion and depression is well documented in books written by others dealing with stroke or other disability and health issues. See Appendix I for those books.

Fortunately, my physicians are well aware of my scenario. They help me out with low dosages of antidepressants. These keep me from sinking into the depths of despair so deep that I cannot see the surface. This assures that I can continue to be a Caregiver and move forward with my life. Also on my side is the fact that I am very aware of the symptoms of depression. When they arrive, I know what they are and most importantly, I know that they will pass. I can function through the momentary plunge into the depression abyss knowing that it is temporary. I am grateful that I truly know the symptoms of depression. Once I meet those symptoms with awareness and mild medication, I can focus on what is really important. I function, let go of the depression, and seek solutions.

※

Moving into acceptance for me has been a rocky process. In most areas, I have been able to accept our new lifestyle with grace and ease. In other areas, specifically the music performance area, I have good days and the occasional bad day when I revert to minor depression. Fortunately my awareness of depression and the steps I take to quell it have not interfered with my spiritual growth. I also do not believe that the occasional step back into tears of mourning necessarily means I have not moved on. Emotions will continue to pop-up now and then, uninvited, experienced, and then allowed to dissipate as I process the feelings that come to the surface. It is all a part of mourning, letting go, and moving forward, one day at a time.

The changes I made, the paradigm shifts I experienced and continue to experience, are now all a part of who I am. I know that I am a much better person from having had all of these experiences. I am grateful that I can now "own" my growth. The process has been long and gradual. I now am able to look back and see the seeds of the "new me" occurring on each step of our journey. My growth is what gives me the ability to face the occasional tears of mourning that erupt because I know those tears are only temporary. They are a very insignificant slice of the richness that is my daily life of thriving in the joy of being a Caregiver.

Everyone's journey through morning is different and dependent upon what individual things you must mourn.

The steps through the process that worked for John and I are specific to our lives as musicians, performers, composers, and artists. It is an individual and unique process. Knowing that you are mourning, and being aware of that process itself helps enormously in the journey through the mourning abyss.

○₰

The most difficult time of year for John and me is the always the Christmas season. As professional musicians, it was always our favorite time of year. We worked extremely hard playing gig after gig of glorious brass Christmas music. It was incredibly joyful to be a part of orchestras, brass quintets, the brass quartet at Universal Studios theme park, and many other venues. For us, nothing says Christmas like the magnificent sounds of brass instruments, echoing throughout splendid cathedrals. We participated in creating that extra special seasonal experience for all those who attended our performances at a multitude of religious ceremonies. The music was always exhilarating and breathtakingly beautiful. We loved every minute of our insane schedules throughout the holiday season.

Since we both lost that part of our performing career, that season now begins annually with us playing our favorite CD of brass Christmas music. We hold hands as the tears run down our faces. It truly feels like we have lost our souls at this time of year. The wound is deep and raw.

There are a few other pieces of music that we hear occasionally that always bring us to tears together. In the classical repertoire, Aaron Copland's "Fanfare for the Common Man" and any Gustav Mahler "Symphony" are particularly poignant for us. Of course the many recordings of our personal performances of John's compositions and his jazz performances tear at our heart strings. Often the scores to film music that bring huge emotional crescendos to the film will bring back tears of regret. All of these elicit the feeling that we were cheated out of years of sharing our skills with the world.

I cannot tell you the number of times people will say to me, are you going to any concerts these days? I tell them, no, I just listen to the music in my head. Those well-meaning people will sometimes continue their queries with, "But music is so joyful, and it fills me with wonderful hopeful feelings! Surely you must want to be a part of that joy! How can you not listen to the pieces of music you loved so much?" I cannot hope to explain to these well-meaning folks that every time I take a seat in an audience, I sit there and try to hide and silence the shaking sobs that quell from my soul as I achingly wish that I was on that stage, giving from within, to produce those beautiful sounds.

However, it will be Christmas again and we will shed a few tears. Then we will take a deep breath, knowing that we were incredibly lucky in our lives to have been able to be a part of the musical world at that level. We also had so much of our performing careers together. We now look back on it from that point of gratitude where it brings us peace, and wait for the next Christmas.

※

Our journey through mourning together

As I have already indicated, the area that has been the most challenging for us to accept was the loss of our careers as professional musicians. John and I moved to Los Angeles and began our careers as professional musicians in 1986. We were both full of joy and so excited. I was accepted as a composer in the University of Southern California's "Composition for the Music Industry" program. That is a long fancy name for "Film Scoring" or writing music for films. I was the first woman ever to be accepted into that program. John and I both knew that being a part of the USC family was one of the best ways to break into the music business in this city. It is all about who you know. This was a gift in our pockets, for me to be at USC.

I knew that it would take me eight to ten years to be accepted into the high level of performance on my instrument, the horn. John would have an easier time of it with about three to five years because there is so much more work for trumpet players. We settled into a routine of writing music and publishing it in our publishing company Trombacor Music. We created about fourteen different music ensembles and actively promoted booking gigs. If we needed specific music for a job, we wrote it.

Our crowning joy was our chamber ensemble called "Rising Winds". John had created the concept for this ensemble in that it included ten players, most of which doubled on other instruments, and all of which were improvisers. This enabled us to perform both classical and jazz style pieces. John wrote most of the music for the group. He started writing music for the ensemble years before we moved to L.A. I contributed a few arrangements. Other members of the ensemble wrote for the group. In order to be eligible for grant funding to build the ensemble, we began the process of creating a Non-Profit Corporation (IRS 501 c3) for Rising Winds. I attended "The Grantsmanship Center" training to become a grant writer for the group. We booked numerous jobs for the ensemble. Its reputation was growing. The State of California graciously accepted our application and granted us our Corporation in early 1991. This was just a couple of months after John's stroke.

We also designed and produced a set of four training VHS videos for beginning instrument players called "Handle With Care". These videos were created to teach how to assemble and care for your new instrument properly. They were manufactured and ready to sell in December of 1990. I developed a series of advertisements for the videos and placed the ads in national magazines that were specific to music educators. They started selling immediately. I was busy shipping videos in January and February of 1991, a mere six weeks before our world crashed.

We were performing, busy, creating, and living our life to its fullest until the stroke. So many hopes, so much skill, so much music to write and perform! We were building the life of our dreams together.

Suddenly we had a lot to mourn. I do not believe that our lives were any more significant than anyone else's who have been touched by catastrophic illness. Everyone who is visited by a life changing event has a lot to mourn. Everyone who is challenged with catastrophic illness has their own line in the sand to step over.

The real tragedy is about the potential that is lost. I often think about the loss to the world of John's incredibly talented trumpet performances and of his skill as a composer. What music did the world not get to experience because of this stroke? What magnificent compositions running around in his head will never be able to get past his aphasia? It is truly a loss.

The tragedy aspect of any loss eventually fades. It becomes more about the change and the acceptance of that change. It is about letting go of the dreams you had previously created and creating new dreams. I have often said that John and I have made a "lot of lemonade" in our lives. It is about living the "paradigm shift".

The truth is, over time it has become clear to both of us that the other side of our line in the sand is knowing that in our hearts and souls, we are both still the artists and musicians that we always were. That will never change. What has changed is that our artistry is only in our hearts. We do not get to share our musical skills with the rest of the world as we had done for so many years. Since his stroke, we have done a couple of very small performances, other than John's job at the church. They are not significant relative to our past skills and careers. We have moved through the mourning stage.

Acceptance is a part of our daily lives. Our flexibility and willingness to change our dreams is what keeps us alive and thriving.

Our dreams now encompass finding joy and laughter in our lives in each moment of the day. We live for the moment, in the moment, because there is no looking back or looking to the future. The future arrives without our concern. We can only experience what is "now". John gets to the end of the day and says, "Good day!" It is not a greeting. He means he had a good day. It is a part of our private world where we live in gratitude for the joy of each moment.

We do miss performing now and then.

Most of the time we live in laughter and gratitude that we were able to give our talents to the world for as long as we could. We have not stopped the music. It is just a different music. Our footprints in the sand are on "the now" side of the line.

Nancy Weckwerth

Soft and Supple

Whatever we do
we do not stiffen
and let the situation make us rigid.

We remain soft and supple
like the branches of a sapling.
Whatever storms may come,
our spirit stays flexible.
Not attached to outcome,
we are not uprooted by the gales.

Rooted, but not rigid,
we move naturally in the winds of change,
bending but never broken.

"The Caregiver's Tao Te Ching" by William and Nancy Martin

Chapter 13

Don't Stop the Music: An Incredible Sense of Purpose

"The purpose of life is to live it, to taste experience to the utmost, to reach out eagerly and without fear for newer and richer experience."

—Eleanor Roosevelt

For Dr. John Swan, music IS his life's purpose–his only one. As long as he has his musical ability, he is happy and living his truth. He knows his talent did not leap out the window with his stroke. Skill and talent are two different realities. John is not concerned that his skills after the stroke are different. He accepts his physical condition. He also believes that what he currently composes is as valid as what he wrote prior to his stroke.

In order to celebrate the incredible sense of purpose, that characterizes Dr. John Swan, I will give a description of his musical life prior to his stroke. The intent of this is to reveal his strength of will, his total commitment to his music, and his inner truth as a way of life. This strength and drive fueled his amazingly fast ascent in his field. He has always known why he was placed on this earth. His joy is in sharing his gifts with the rest of the world. Always looking for that new and richer experience, John has followed his muse and moved to many different cities. A brief account of his pre-stroke life-journey follows.

ଊ

John's life story: pre-stroke

John D. Swan, DMA, (Doctor of Musical Arts) grew up in Toronto, Ontario, Canada. He started playing trumpet when he was thirteen years old. At the young age of fifteen, he had his first professional job playing dance music. He graduated from high school and earned his A.R.C.T. or Associate of the Royal Conservatory in Toronto in trumpet performance. This is an organization modeled on the Royal Conservatory in London, England. He received his Bachelor's Degree in Music Education from the University of Toronto. He then traveled to New Haven, Connecticut and received his Master's degree in trumpet performance from Yale University. Following that success, he accepted a position as the Head of the Music Department at the "Iolani School" in Honolulu, Hawaii. While in Honolulu, he became the principal trumpet player of the Honolulu Symphony, now the Hawaii Symphony. From there he accepted faculty teaching positions at the University of British Columbia in Vancouver, B.C., the University of Western Ontario in London, Ontario, and Florida Atlantic University in Boca Raton, Florida. John received his Doctor of Musical Arts degree, (DMA) from the University of Miami in Coral Gables, Florida, in music composition. While in Florida he became one of the staff composers for Columbia Pictures Publications. Columbia Pictures Publications was eventually purchased by Warner Brothers, which is a typical occurrence in the music publishing industry. John's extensive work for them is now all out of print.

During all of these situations, John was performing in each city as a freelance musician in both the classical and jazz fields. He is one of a few very rare musicians who does both at an extremely high level. He wrote music for many organizations and groups. His compositional skills were and still are astounding: he writes continuously.

One particularly interesting use of this skill was when he and I were on the road travelling with the Mantovani Orchestra throughout the United States. A singer had arrived to perform with the orchestra and the music he brought with him for the orchestra was actually for a big band. It was the wrong instrumentation for the Mantovani Orchestra which is mostly strings and a few brass and woodwinds. Overnight in our hotel room with no keyboard, John rewrote the entire piece for the correct instruments while I copied the musical parts for the players. The next morning at the rehearsal, the orchestra members played straight through the work–there was not one error. By nightfall, it was performed on stage.

After John and I became a team in the music world, we created our own publishing company called Trombacor Music. We both wrote and arranged for our self-publishing endeavor. The catalog, with distribution in Germany and the United States, contains nearly one hundred items which are still used by numerous small ensembles. Together we wrote a full length ballet for full orchestra. This work was submitted to the International Ballet Composition Competition in Geneva, Switzerland where it was one of the top three contenders. John and I took Trombacor Music Publishing to the International Trumpet Guild conventions as vendors several times. We were fortunate to sell many copies of our compositions at these events. At one of those, I recall the representative from Ludwig Publishing calling us "The Gold Dust Twins."

Three years after we got together, John and I moved to Los Angeles to become a part of the music world in this fabulous city. Five years after we arrived, John had his stroke at the age of fifty-three. Although the stroke changed the circumstances of his daily life, it has not dulled his incredible sense of purpose.

☙

On a sense of purpose coupled with quality of life for a person who is disabled

There are really only two situations pertaining to quality of life and happiness in the life of a person who is disabled. The first is when someone is born with a disability. Second is when someone becomes disabled at some point in their life after birth. In each case, the quality of life and happiness issues are different.

In the first case, since the person was born with the disability, hopefully they have discovered things to do that they enjoy. They do not compete with the ghost of their former life without the disability held over their heads. They may not even see themselves as disabled. If they had good parenting where they were taught that they have value for who they are, it simply IS who they are. Their purpose in life has always been defined by their disability. What they enjoy may be something entirely different than the rest of us could even imagine. It matters not for it brings them happiness and joy.

Someone who becomes disabled in life due to disease or accident after early childhood without a disability has a different challenge. They may be faced with having to change what they felt was their sense of purpose in life. They may have to make more lemonade because the ghost of previous joy lives within them. Based upon their new individual physical or mental challenges, they may have to let go of their previous purpose and find a new one.

In either situation, it becomes the Caregiver's opportunity to help discover what makes the highest quality of life possible for a person with a disability. It is a voyage of exploration. It is like writing a new symphony for that person. In addition, if the Caregiver can move into viewing it as their personal purpose to provide quality of life for their loved one and consequently for themselves, it is their proof that they have succeeded twofold. Looking at this task as an opportunity for the Caregiver puts an entirely different spin on the issue of quality of life. The very word, "opportunity", is all about hope, creativity, progress, and other emotions based on love, not fear. The success is for the loved one and for the personal growth of the Caregiver.

ॐ

I truly believe that thinking in terms of providing quality of life, not merely maintenance or daily care, is what brings quality of life to both the disabled person and to the Caregiver. That is the joy. Life is about change. Accepting that paradigm shift or that change, and building upon it is what brings joy to both Caregiver and Survivor. Daily care and maintenance of the Survivor's needs become merely a background stepping stone to the real activities of every day. These real activities provide the true quality of life for both members of the team.

It is pointless to look back at your previous life and ask the Universe for that life back. It cannot happen. We cannot go backwards in time.

We have two choices in life. We can either do things well or we can do things poorly. We get to choose. By choosing to do things well after a disabling event of any kind, we allow the brain to think in terms of solutions rather than wallowing in despair. Despair gives no one quality of life. A sense of purpose is the process of forward motion. Once we move forward, we live with hope. We have fun. We heal. We live in joy.

※

To start, here is a list of questions that I as Caregiver asked about John that helped me move in the direction of finding solutions and reuniting him with his sense of purpose:

1. What made him happy prior to becoming disabled?
2. What will make him happy now?
3. What does John need to give him the opportunity to fulfill item two above?
4. How can I provide the items he needs to fulfill item two?

Why is it the Caregiver's opportunity to provide those gifts that makes item two possible?

My answers to the above questions for John are as follows:

1. Playing his trumpet and writing music.
2. Playing his trumpet and writing music. (Note it is the same, and we both know it.)
3. I provided trumpets that are modified so that he can hold them in one hand: his left. He also has a piano or a keyboard to use for writing music.
4. The "how" is about finding ways to make item number three happen logistically and financially. For me, finding an instrument repair person who could modify his trumpets was critical. Finding and purchasing an electronic keyboard that was simple enough to use was also important. Learning new things is challenging for John. He would need to learn how to turn on this keyboard, change sounds, and turn it off. Teaching him to use the keyboard was also part of "the how".

Depending upon the severity of the Survivor's mental condition, it becomes the Caregiver's responsibility to discover and make these things happen because the Survivor may no longer be able to do so.

Once I had this handle on the answers to the questions, I sealed them in my memory. I wish I would have kept a journal. A journal would have been a reference to review as time flowed forward. Journals help you remember your great thoughts and one certainly does not want to forget any of those! Now I knew what direction I was going and I began to look for the solutions that would give John the highest quality of life possible. I also made mental notes regarding changes and growth in the items that John needed to improve his quality of life.

༄

On my first goal: providing reconnection to his incredible sense of purpose

As Caregiver, I felt it was my purpose to find a way to reconnect John to his life's purpose. It was at about thirty days after his stroke that I brought him a trumpet mouthpiece to see what would happen. He took it in his now only good hand, his left, and placed it on his lips. He blew through it and behold, sound came out. Rejoice! I knew we were going to be OK. The next task was to find a way for him to hold his trumpet. Trumpeters typically use both hands—the left to hold the trumpet and the right to push down on the fingering valves. John now had only one useable hand. I took his horns into an instrument repair person and had them altered so that he could hold and finger using his left hand only.

He now began what I considered the painstaking process of learning to play his instrument with his other hand. If you are right handed, imagine learning to perform all of your daily tasks with your left hand. I will not go in to the brain skills involved in doing this. John, however, was undaunted. He started practicing every day and taught his left hand the skills of fingering the different notes on the trumpet. This required building this skill as if he were a total beginner. The muscle memory normally involved in this takes years to develop, especially to the level of a professional performer. Not for John. After a year, he was developing real agility with his left hand. He did not have time to be angry or depressed. He had a mission. He had purpose.

If I could count the number of days in his life that John has not played his trumpet, I would place money on the fact that it was maybe less than ten days a year, since he was thirteen years old. This of course was until he was hospitalized with the stroke. Once he was firmly back on the road to recovery at home, he began his daily practice ritual again. He lives to practice every day. This personal dedication to developing and maintaining his talent made him an amazing performer.

For those readers who are not musicians, playing a brass instrument such as a trumpet, is like being a sports professional. The performer must exercise (practice) daily to keep in good physical shape to perform at the top of their game. If you do not practice daily, you will have problems with stamina, accuracy, and technique.

On his own judgment of his quality of life

How does one measure the quality of one's own life? How does one discover this incredible sense of purpose? I believe that the two go hand in hand. Each person's life's purpose is fulfilled when they have the quality of life they desire. For John, all he has ever wanted is to play his trumpet and write music. Everything else is secondary. This attitude is what made him a truly fine musician in the first place. By providing this opportunity for him, John still is living the life of his dreams. He is living his "incredible sense of purpose." Anyone could argue that he lost a career as a fine musician. But in his eyes and ears, he still is a fine musician. One of the blessings of the stroke is that it took away his ability to judge that his performance level and therefore his career is different. He truly enjoys just practicing his instrument at home and writing music. That has become his new career.

He still writes music every day. He has completed many "works of art" in his eyes in the past twenty-five years. He loves each composition and has me play it for him on the piano. He writes string quartets, brass quintets, brass quartets, and other works of chamber music for small ensembles. For a while, I helped him create computerized sound scores so he could hear them on his own. This became too difficult for his brain to process. Teaching John how to use the computer for notating music is almost another chapter. We left that tool on the launch pad very soon after we started it. At one point, I created individual performance parts for a couple of his compositions and they were performed.

The quality of what he writes now is vastly different than the magnificent works he composed prior to his stroke. He often struggles with some of the minute details of notating what he composes. However, he absolutely knows what he wants. When he finishes a composition, he always asks me to play the score for him on the piano. I find the notation errors, and ask him what he wants. He tells me what is correct, and I fix the notation.

Before his stroke, John had over one hundred published compositions with multiple publishing companies. He was well known as a composer in South Florida, Toronto, and Los Angeles. His doctoral thesis, a music composition, is still in our garage. I do not have the heart to throw it away. Many of his personal style techniques still appear in each composition. Their quality relative to his past works does not really matter. To him, they are magnificent works now. Who is to judge? In reality, the fact that he can complete works of this nature at all is proof to me that they are indeed magnificent works. Small miracles daily make for a fabulous quality of life for John. His success is in his eyes. He is simply not interested in the world's opinions.

John wakes up every morning, looks forward to the day, and plans his practice time. He delights in giving me a report of "seventy percent today" when he stops practicing. Some days, he is really excited and says "A hundred percent, yes, a hundred percent today." It is his method of judging how he sounded, how easy it was, and what he accomplished in his trumpet practice session. He feels tremendously successful. You can see it in his face and hear it in his voice. I cannot tell you how grateful I am that he feels successful.

After John practices his trumpet he naps, has lunch, naps again, and then goes to the piano to write music for over an hour. Often when I have left the house for work and come home, he is waiting to tell me "Finished my piece!" He has probably written over two hundred pieces in the last twenty five years.

A good friend of mine is a specialist in training Special Education Teachers. Over the years we have had numerous discussions about brain damage and its effect on the human condition. As an expert in the field, I believe she told me that it is quite common for people with brain injuries to believe that they are the same as they always were in most aspects of their life. They may not always comprehend how disabled they are. Therefore John's opinion of his skills may be a common result of brain damage. Whether that is truly the case here, or that John's incredible sense of purpose is what is ruling his opinion of himself, is irrelevant. He believes–his life has purpose. He is full of joy every day and lives in gratitude that he awakens each day. What a blessing this is.

CR

Anyone can look at others and see that they are happy, joyous, or loving. However, no one can make them that way or live their path for them. Nor can anyone else live your path for you. As John's Caregiver, I have merely facilitated his reconnection to what he knew before his stroke and what he knows now. He lives his "incredible sense of purpose" every day. He has a very high quality of life. My joy arises from knowing that I have done the best job I could possibly do, most of the time. I did this based upon what I knew at the moment. It became my joy to create the opportunity for him to have joy in his life.

I have learned much about success and quality of life from John. The most important thing I have learned is that the only person who can determine your success in life, your joy, your quality of life, is you. No one else has either the right or the criteria to make that decision for you. Watching John grow as a person and improve as a musician (on the level he is on) is evidence of his quality of life.

ଔ

On personal dignity for John: another aspect of quality of life

Personal dignity is extremely important for all human beings. John was still a young man at the time of his stroke. He was fifty-three when it happened and life changed for him. In the first new home I purchased, the bathroom in his practice studio had a corner shower stall that allowed John to bathe himself. It was just large enough to hold a shower seat. I had a handheld shower head installed. The room was about five feet by five feet in size. With the shower stall, small sink and toilet, there was barely enough room to turn around. That meant there was no way for him to even fall and hurt himself. He could not fall far enough to get to the floor. This gave him the much needed dignity of being able to attend to his own personal hygiene. It also gave me the tremendous freedom to not have to bathe him daily. More importantly, it gave me the peace of mind knowing that he was as safe as possible in the bathroom when I was not home.

John is not particularly aware of how important it is for him to be able to take care of his own personal needs. First, John does not care about how he looks. He is a musician through and through. As long as he has a trumpet, a pencil and music paper, his world is full. Second, John likes to be taken care of by others in many aspects of life. He is basically not a responsible person to anything other than his music. Again, he is a musician. I have always known this was his personality. I also knew that those personality traits are what made him "great."

When I sold our first home and moved to a temporary apartment in another city, we had to change the pattern of his daily bath. The apartment has a bathtub. Even with a shower seat sitting in the tub, he cannot get in and out of a bathtub on his own. He cannot lift his weak leg over the edge. The day after we moved into the apartment, we developed an easy technique of me assisting with getting him in and out of the tub. We laugh and sing as we do this in order to keep his fear level down.

Singing is amazing! I highly recommend it. When we sing simple songs during his bath, John forgets how frightening it is. He has a fear of falling in the tub. The more fearful he becomes—the stiffer his body becomes. Then it gets more difficult to maneuver safely in and out of the tub. When we start singing, it achieves at least two things: (1) He has to breathe so he cannot hold his breath and therefore he does not get so stiff. (2) We giggle. Before he even realizes what has happened, he is out of the tub getting his rub down with towels and then lotion.

The quality of John's life achieved here is that of giggles and laughs while bathing, even if he is being assisted. We have lowered the fear factor immensely. As he is now in his middle seventies, he is facing the normal results of aging. We should all be so lucky to be singing and giggling like six-year-olds while taking a bath at this age. Oh, we have a yellow rubber ducky sitting on the shelf in the bathroom to remind us that life should always be a Lark, 'er Duck. John's nickname when he was a professor in college was "Dr. Duck", a play on his real name, "Dr. Swan". How lucky we are!

Dressing Apraxia, a term used for one type of outcome that occurs with stroke, is an interesting phenomenon. For example, most of the time John is able to dress himself without assistance. However, every once in a while, he gets himself tangled in an article of clothing and cannot figure out how to solve the problem. This was more prevalent in the first few years after his stroke. Anymore, it only happens if he is really tired.

Conceptual Apraxia is an inability to remember how to use simple daily tools like silverware. John still tries to eat soup with a fork now and then. I am grateful John has so few of these common symptoms. None of these are serious safety issues that I have to be concerned about when I leave him home alone. He actually seems to do better when I am not there. His self-sufficient attitude gives him a higher quality of life.

As a Caregiver, I constantly watch over John as if he were a toddler. I try to be as unobtrusive as possible as I watch in order to give John his personal dignity because he is an adult. This helps maintain his sense of self-worth, and his sense of purpose. I watch for ways to improve his quality of life as I look for solutions to situations as they arise. Simple solutions for maintaining personal dignity often go a long way.

Simple Solutions to Create Quality of Life

I keep a small gift bag with handles near his favorite chair in the living room. If he wants to carry a snack or a different pair of glasses, he can put those items in the small bag. This allows him to carry such items in his good hand while also holding his cane as he walks.

When I am going to be gone for the day, I make his lunch and put it in the refrigerator. I take a plastic grocery bag and hang it on the refrigerator handle for him to carry his sandwich to his table. Again, he has only one hand and that one is using a cane. A method of carrying items is essential. I keep looking for a small piece of furniture with wheels that he could push with his cane that would act as a moving tray. So far I have had no luck on finding the right piece of furniture that would work for him. A walker does not work because of his one handed use. He leans on one side and they can tip over. His walking method does not allow for any risk-taking.

John has difficulty walking in from outside and closing the door behind him. I do not use automatic door closers because they will slam the door against him and knock him over. I know they can be adjusted. I have found that adjustment to be unreliable because John's walking is inconsistent. In order for him to come into a door, I hang a two foot piece of rope on the inside handle. Then as he comes in the door, he holds the rope as he walks in and pulls the door with him at his own speed. He is still working on learning this technique. Learning a new skill such as this is very challenging for him.

If a tin can had to be opened for a meal, I used only cans that had a pull tab on them for many years. Now, I have to open all cans before I leave the house and put the people-food or cat-food in another container that he can use. John is not able to make a judgment himself about what is microwavable. Plastic containers with lids are the best solution. At one time, I purchased a one handed can-opener online that is for opening cans without pull tabs. I do not recommend it. It was expensive. It worked by removing the entire top of the can. This left a raw sharp edge on the can. This is far too dangerous for John to use.

The only shoes that John can use by himself are those with Velcro closers. These are challenging to find in stores. They can be purchased online or from mail order catalogs. Some discount department stores also carry those sneakers with Velcro closers. They tend to be discount in quality as well. They last only about a year and do not offer a lot of support for John's walking issues. Since they are "discount" shoes, it is not expensive to toss them when the sole breaks off and purchase a new pair.

I now purchase some clothing on the Internet for John. There are online stores that feature clothing for people with disabilities. These articles of clothing are designed for comfort while sitting in wheelchairs or for ease of getting dressed using Velcro. Such clothing is often made without seams that cause discomfort when sitting on that seam in a wheelchair for long periods of time. Any Internet search engine will help you find those stores. I recommend trying out one item first to test the quality of the item before you replace an entire wardrobe.

All of the solutions above are examples of things a Caregiver must find for someone with a brain injury. These solutions are not earth shattering nor do they exhibit extreme cleverness. The intention is to exemplify the process of how to seek out solutions. John is not mentally capable of finding these solutions or of shopping. Neither can he implement their use without some practice and re-learning of skills. I believe all of these solutions are an opportunity for the Caregiver to problem solve and seek solutions for each particular situation.

The Caregiver is the merely a catalyst for the sense of purpose for the Survivor. The Survivor guides their own life with loving support and guidance provided by the Caregiver.

Every solution I found, whether it was for the personal dignity of his self-care, or the personal dignity of facilitating his reconnection to his music, was gratifying for both John and for me. Both types of dignity are what it takes to give him the best possible quality of life so that he can live his life's purpose.

Finding these solutions also makes my caregiving a lighter job each day. When I find a way to make John's life a little better, my life gets better, too. This is why I constantly observe John's day, his behaviors, and what he has to do. When I see a problem, or I see him struggling to do something, I choose to find a way to improve upon his process. Then it is a win-win situation. That is how we find the joy: in re-discovering John's life purpose together.

On having a sense of purpose together

John and I have been best friends for over thirty-five years. I knew him first from his reputation as one of the finest musicians in the south Florida area. My knowledge of his reputation preceded our meeting by several years. We met in the local orchestras and became friends as fellow musicians. Several years into our friendship, his second marriage broke up. During that breakup, John began dating another musician. He and I were already close friends, largely because of the mutual level of our skills as performers. John was the principal trumpet player in the orchestra in which we worked, and I was the principal horn player. That meant we typically sat next to one another in rehearsals and performances. Along the way he got divorced, stopped dating the other musician, and he and I grew together as musicians and friends.

One rather humorous event occurred while we were performing in the Palm Beach Opera one season. In this rather strange performing venue, John sat directly behind me. The entire orchestra was on the main floor, next to the audience. A stage was built about four feet above the floor due to the nature of the venue. This placed the orchestra in between the stage and the audience, but on the same level as the audience. There was only a walking path for the musicians and conductor between the orchestra and audience. As is typical in many performance situations, the same season ticket holders always had the same seats. There was a row of the "blue rinse set" that always sat right next to us for the Sunday Matinees. Their seats were less than three feet away from us. One afternoon, just before the Overture, one of the gals leaned over and whispered in my ear, "Did you ever marry that man who sits behind you?" I was flabbergasted! They had been watching our friendship grow for years. I laughed and replied, "You know, we are getting married in a few weeks!" That was in December of 1982. We were married in January of 1983. That was when our sense of purpose together began.

08

After over twenty-five years of being a stroke Survivor, John still practices his trumpet and writes music daily. His belief in his skill is rewarding to watch. There are currently boxes of compositions that he has written since his stroke. He completes a work, puts it away, and starts another.

John is a testament to acceptance and a successful recovery because he never looks back, only forward, living his life each day, in each moment. He knows how he needs to live: he has not stopped the music.

Learn from them

It is not necessary to intrude,
nor do we have to meddle.
People can be trusted with their lives.
Even when we may feed them,
bathe them,
and clothe them,
we do not lead their lives for them.
They lead their lives themselves.

In everything we do
we leave a space for them.
They alone know what to do,
how to live,
when to hold on,
when to struggle,
and when to let go.

"The Caregiver's Tao Te Ching" by William and Nancy Martin.

Chapter 14

A Triumph of Spirit: A New Kind of Music

The transition from musician to Caregiver

Almost everyone I listen to has a very interesting life. From the moment we are born, the events that occur shape our hopes, dreams, and goals. Add to that the force of the unknown with circumstances beyond our control and it becomes a story. Everyone has a story to tell. The older I get the more I see the value in listening to the stories of others. It is such a rewarding experience because I get to learn from others.

On the topic of learning, the people that I find the most interesting to be around are those who are willing to grow and learn. Those people pique my interest. They challenge me, I learn from them.

One of my friends once said to me, "life is what happens when you're making other plans." Although I did not know it at the time, I now know that my friend was quoting lyrics from John Lennon's "Beautiful Boy

(Darling Boy)". I learned an important lesson from her comment. The lesson is to be aware that life is always changing. It is always moving one through unexpected paths. There is no guarantee that what one plans for, what one's goals are, or what one prepares oneself for via education will actually materialize. Her statement to me was profound because it caused a paradigm shift in my personal awareness process. What a gift it is to learn from someone else. She changed my life with her comment.

The purpose of this chapter is to trace my own growth and my learning throughout the process of the events that have occurred in relation to the story of my friend and partner, John Swan. I do not think that my life is particularly different or more book-worthy than anyone else's story. I do believe that the process of growth holds merit. The merit that I see is the profound spiritual change that has occurred in me, and as I write is still occurring.

I truly believe that we are each a spirit having an earthly experience in a body. The purpose of this experience is to heal. When I consider where I started on this journey, and where I am now, I cannot believe the lessons I have learned. All of the lessons helped me heal. I am incredibly grateful that I was given this opportunity to share the events of John's life with him. Together we have survived and now, more importantly we thrive!

After I graduated from high school in Minnesota, I attended college for two years at Concordia College in Moorhead, MN. I also attended the two summer sessions after both years so at the beginning of my third year of college, I was a senior. I majored in Latin with a Liberal Arts Major in Music. After some soul searching and an amazing experience at a jazz summer camp in Wisconsin, I transferred for my third full year of college to the University of Wisconsin, at Eau Claire. I graduated from UWEC with a Bachelor's Degree in Music Education. After that I began teaching music with Music for America, Inc. in Elkhart, Indiana. Music for America was a division of the Selmer and Bach Corporation that manufactures brass and woodwind instruments. They hired teachers to go into smaller private music schools that could not afford to have a music program. Under their umbrella, I created brand new music programs in seven small schools.

Dissatisfied with teaching elementary school music, I asked the company if they had a high school somewhere. They said they had a high school in Miami so I packed my piano, horn, cat, and all my other belongings in a U-Haul trailer and moved to Miami. In the fall of that year, I started teaching in two private Catholic schools in Miami. The high school backed out of the program so I was again unhappy with my teaching job.

Don't Stop the Music

While I was teaching there, I applied and was accepted into the Master of Music program at the University of Miami in Coral Gables. I graduated with my Master's degree in Applied Music or Performance on my instrument, the horn. During this time I was already working as a professional musician in the Greater Miami area. My first professional job was with the Florida Philharmonic as an extra horn for Gustav Mahler's "Symphony No. 1." On my first professional gig as a musician, I performed a symphony by my most favorite composer of all time! How wonderful!

In addition to performing music in Miami, which was a six month a year job, I earned my Real Estate license in Florida. I needed something to do for the other six months of the year for income. This was a fun and easy career. I had a great time, sold some houses, and made a little money (actually, very little money). House prices were low and interest rates were in the fifteen per-cent range. Remember those days? That interest rate certainly scared off a lot of buyers so my business was rather slow to grow.

Somewhere in time within the next couple of years, John and I met while performing in the Palm Beach Orchestra. The rest of my career story parallels John's so it has already been related. In other chapters I have also cited how John and I worked together, up until the stroke, building our careers in the music business. We moved from the Miami area, to Toronto, and then to

Los Angeles where I was accepted at the University of Southern California in their film scoring program as a composer. I graduated with a Certificate in Composition for the Music Industry just two years prior to John's stroke.

In the Los Angeles area, I free-lanced as a musician. I composed a lot of music, published a lot of music, and John and I were building our dream career. To have some stable income, I accepted a position at a local retail store that was quite close to our rented house in southern California.

After John's stroke in 1991, my first career move was to give myself full-time status at the retail store where I was the manager of a department. We needed the guaranteed income. I was fortunate in that they needed me to do that anyway. My main duty was as the buyer of all product.

For the first two and a half years after John's stroke, I bravely tried to continue practicing my instrument. I accepted music performance gigs as I could. Those gigs dwindled as my skill as a performer gradually slipped because my duties as Caregiver consumed my time. I even gave a couple of recitals in churches and at local concert venues.

I did not know at this point that our lives had experienced a paradigm shift – a change of no-return. There was no going back. This lesson was staring me in the face but I was not yet ready to learn it. This paradigm shift was a piece of my puzzle that I was not ready to pick up yet. I still believed we could go back to our previous lifestyle.

> **LESSON LEARNED**
>
> In retrospect, I realize that throughout these early years my transformation from musician to Caregiver was a gradual process of which I was unaware. This realization was trickling into my days as if a tiny scissors was snipping away at the fabric of my soul. Each miniscule thread was not really missed at the moment. However, the unraveling of my career continued—one missed day of practice at a time.

I left the retail store after John had been disabled for three years. My departure was timed so that future insurance companies could not deny him coverage based upon a pre-existing condition. In order to find better paying work, I started with a temporary agency. While working one temporary job, I was offered a full-time position at a university campus in their music library. This was particularly profound for me. It was now five years after his stroke and for the first time, while in that library, I was able to listen to music again.

Until my time in the music library, it was so painful for me to listen to music that I just turned off the music in my head and in my heart. It brought me to tears to hear a Mahler symphony, or any symphony, opera, or ballet music. I sobbed whenever I heard a jazz trumpet player. It became easier to never turn on the radio at home or in the car. I ceased listening to our large collection of albums and compact discs. I never attended performances of music of any kind because I could not stop the shaking and crying.

While I was at work at the music library, I was often alone in the library for hours upon end. I finally found the courage to begin listening to music again. There was no one to witness my total emotional collapse as the long pent up tears of grieving began to flow.

During all the varied career changes, the struggle to manage John's care and our survival financially, I felt my musical energy dissipating into mediocrity. My prior drive to be a musician with that intense focus needed to perform at the level to which I was accustomed was sinking into the near-distant past. Caregiving fatigue drove my ability to be a professional musician into a deep dark abyss. I knew from within my soul that I simply could no longer do it all well. Even as my heart was breaking, I knew that something had to change. I also stopped composing music. Little by little, my practice time on the horn was usurped by the financial needs of our household.

I struggled with letting go of the concept that my career as a professional musician was over. This loss of my hard-earned career as a musician was more than I could endure. I realized that I was assembling my life and my emotions like pieces of a large puzzle. So many pieces did not fit. The music pieces of my life felt as if they belonged to a different picture puzzle on the living room table. These pieces no longer seemed to fit into the income-creation-person I was becoming out of necessity.

Agonizingly, I admitted to myself that the most unproductive and financially unhelpful use of my time was in trying to maintain our dream ensemble, Rising Winds, and my performance skills. The stabbing pain this caused in my soul sometimes still recurs.

To quell the pain of the impending decision to stop the music for me, I made a promise to myself. My agreement was that I would quit music for five years to focus on first making us financially stable. If at the end of the five years, I was content with where I was, I would allow myself to consider going back to being a musician as an option, not a requirement. My happiness in whatever the future held would be the deciding factor. If I was truly unhappy and we were financially stable, I would wholeheartedly jump back into the world of professional performance. If I was happy in what I was doing, then I gave myself permission to stay where I was. I finally stopped the music. Or at least, music as I knew it at the time.

Surprisingly, this decision and process gave me freedom. I had let go of the past desire to perform music on a high professional level that was dragging my energy into that black abyss. I could now think about how I needed to proceed. I had to let go of the past in order to move forward and grow. I needed to find a new way to make music.

In order to solve the issue of what I would do to make us financially stable, my first question to myself was: "What else are you doing now, that you enjoy." My answer was, "Working on the computer".

While I was at the university, I was offered a step-up position in a computer lab. Based upon my computer skills that had been honed while creating databases in the music library, I became the manager of one of the computer labs on the campus. My salary doubled. By this time, I had full PPO health insurance for both John and I. For the first time, I reached another one of my goals. That important goal was to provide quality health insurance for John and me. While working on the campus, with John in tow on site most of the time, I was able to build additional computer skills.

LESSON LEARNED

It was at about the 10 year anniversary of John's stroke when another piece of the puzzle fell into place for me. I realized that I had just spent ten years putting out fires and finding solutions to the challenges that occurred each day. The puzzle piece that was called caregiving was now more than just something I did each

> day—it had become a way of life. I released the old "Musician" me and had moved into a new space called "Caregiver" me. This was a huge paradigm shift for me. It was the next step towards moving into a space where I approached caregiving more often from a point of loving, rather than that of firefighter. This shift in my consciousness made my days lighter and easier. More importantly the shift paved the way for even greater spiritual growth for me.

One day, a music faculty member walked into the computer lab and told me about an even better job with her husband who owned a "dot-com" startup. I interviewed with the husband. He offered me the job with a great salary, better benefits, and the whole enchilada. I grabbed the opportunity to improve my salary and began the now longer commute on the public transportation system. Three months later, the venture capitalist that had funded this dot-com was shut down by the U.S. Securities and Exchange Commission (SEC). Abruptly, my job disappeared!

The Cloud Fear *has set in again as I am jobless with no income. Now I am carrying mortgage payments in addition to caring for John. I am so extremely insecure about my skills because I am beginning to feel like a dilatant. I have too many skills in disparate careers. None of my employment experience is in my degree fields.*

Plus I am in my late forties and I am afraid of age-related discrimination in the hiring field.

Throughout all of this, my overall goal had always been to provide the best quality of life possible for John. I now believed I had achieved that! He enjoyed each and every day, doing what he wanted to do. I decided it was my turn—my next goal was to provide quality of life for me.

I feel as if this goal is in alignment within my soul. But how do I achieve this for me? What is it I really want? I am floundering between jobs again, with unemployment benefits expiring, the impending bill crunch is extremely frightening for me.

After being out of work for six months, I was offered a new full-time position at the same university branch I had left nine months earlier. My new webmaster job was to build websites for nine different departments in the university. I was in heaven. I got to make digital videos of concerts, theatre and dance performances and put it all on the web. It was creativity central for me.

After about a year of the webmaster position, the financial crisis in the State of California caused budget cuts in the California State University System and my job as webmaster disappeared. I seemed to be trapped in a circus of disappearing jobs.

To relay this "wonderful" news, I was invited to a meeting with the administrators. They informed me that my job was disappearing. Because they knew both John and me and wanted to provide income and insurance for us, they relayed that they would do their best to keep me employed until I found another job. They were extremely kind to me. Instead of kicking me out the door unceremoniously and instantly, they agreed to find a way to create a win-win situation for all of us. What unbelievable kindness and good luck!

In a moment of absolute divine inspiration after their news, I mentioned that since I had a Master's degree, I could actually teach for them. The folks in the meeting looked at each other and had one of those "A-HA" moments. They realized they could use me in a faculty position that served them and me. I began teaching an Introduction to Music class and became a faculty advisor for the Arts and Letters Department. I also designed and taught online classes for the College of Arts and Letters and for the Music Department. I was able to extend the position on this campus for another nine months or so while I was looking for another job.

For my 50th birthday, I bought myself a new car: a 2001 Ford Mustang. This was the car of my childhood dreams. I remember the most beautiful baby blue Mustang convertibles of the 60's. This self-indulgence was not out of excess, I really needed a new car. I decided the next half century of my life would be in "fun" cars, not practical ones. This was the first step in adding quality to my life! My new purchase was a beautiful coupe that is forest green with teal blue undercoating. It glitters in the sun.

The Road Trip that went along with this purchase included nabbing two girlfriends and speeding to Las Vegas for the weekend. Ah, respite. We laughed, ate, sampled some not-so-good wine, and of course, played on the slot machines. To her surprise, one of my gal-pals had an old boy-friend show up to meet her there. This weekend was an escape in more ways than one.

I found out a couple of weeks later that when she went home after our weekend, she had asked her husband to leave. As a result of this challenging change for her husband, he learned about a series of personal growth seminars provided by a company called "Insight Seminars". He told me about the first seminar and suggested I take it. I did so in 2002. To this day, I feel his suggestion was the finest thing any friend has ever done for me. It still amazes me how the challenges and opportunities life weaves for all of us are interwoven. Happy Accidents are everywhere.

Another piece of the puzzle appeared after taking the "Insight I" seminar. This personal growth training gave me tools into a world of self-confidence and personal success that I never knew existed. It was the beginning of a real quest into adding a new layer of spirituality in my life. I was awakening into a transformed "me."

Don't Stop the Music

> If you wish to learn more about the Insight Seminars, the Internet link to further information is in Appendix III.

My job search included filling out an online application for a faculty position at a local technical college. I promptly forgot about it. Several weeks later in late spring, I got a phone call from the campus Associate Dean. He asked me if I could interview in about two hours. With eyes very wide open to the point of bugging out in shock, I asked if I could be there in early afternoon. I scrambled into interview attire, grabbed a résumé, and drove to the campus. After greeting the Associate Dean, the next words out of his mouth were, "These are the classes I need you to teach, starting in five days. Please look at them and tell me which ones you can handle. We'll do the interview later." I selected two classes on his list. He was relieved, we did an interview and paperwork was signed. We negotiated a part time position while I was completing classes I was currently teaching at the university. It was an amazing opportunity for everyone. Talk about win-win-win situations. I was incredibly grateful. I was teaching three classes at the university, and two classes at the technical college.

There was an extremely interesting challenge for me at the technical college as I learned more about my new job. One of the classes I was assigned to teach in computer animation required knowledge of a software application that I had never used before. I literally raced home, got on the Internet, and enrolled in a 2-day weekend class in the specific software in San Francisco. I quickly booked a flight, a hotel, and got on a plane on Saturday. That was two days before my job started.

I returned home from the training class on Sunday evening. I arrived at my new job on Monday morning at 8:00 a.m., a mere nine hours before I was supposed to teach a class on this software. Be advised here, that I had plenty of experience in the topic I was hired to teach. I had taught animation in the computer lab at the university. It was just a different software application. When I arrived on the campus, I was confident in my very fresh skills in Version 5 of the particular software that I had learned over the weekend. Once I booted up the campus computer lab software and looked at the textbook, I discovered that the curriculum and software on the campus called for one version back, Version 4. Additionally, the campus textbook was in Version 3. Since the software company had done a major overhaul of the software between Version 3 and 4, nothing in the campus software or the textbook matched my Version 5 skills. Even their textbook and the lab software did not work together! I now had eight hours to design a class for my students. I decided that I was nothing, if not flexible. So I delved into the software the campus owned and created classes for the entire quarter based upon the software tutorials and text on hand in their lab.

This kind of challenge perpetuated throughout the next three years that I worked for the technical college. They continued to ask me to step outside of my knowledge base and excel. I remember one quarter when I was teaching nine courses. This was a total of forty-five college-level units. All nine of the classes had brand new textbooks and curriculum. Everything I had done for the previous several quarters became irrelevant. The schedule they devised for me was so intense that I could not even take time off to fly to Minnesota for my niece's wedding. There was no one to cover my classes. Campus rules included a "no class cancelation" policy and there were no substitute teachers available. This was perhaps my biggest regret: I missed that wonderful family event.

I know that the students at this campus were thrilled with me as a teacher. I pushed them above and beyond their expectations because I was always pushing myself. If I could do it, so could they. I set the bar extremely high for them. Many times I heard at the end of the semester "Ms. W (my faculty nom de plume on campus), I worked harder than I have ever worked in my life for you, but I have also learned more than I have ever learned. Thank you!" Ten and more years later, I still get emails from grateful students. I am thankful I got the opportunity to have such a tremendous effect upon so many people. Teaching is an incredibly rewarding career.

CR

I am totally exhausted. This ultra-intense job is causing mental burnout for me. How am I going to continue with my normal teaching day—either one or two five hour classes, six days a week? Each of these classes includes homework grading, test grading, lesson plans, and faculty-duty hours in the campus library.

Now they have added online teaching to my load! That means I spend one to two hours a day grading online work and monitoring student email and collaborative assignments. The online class is in addition to my regular class load.

I feel the **Fear** *returning, but this time it is the fear that I will collapse into severe fatigue or worse yet, into illness from this overwhelming teaching load.*

I feel as if I am merely surviving each day. I am also trying to build a secure financial life for us. Survival includes doing everything possible each day until I collapse in bed at the end of the day. The monumental career and skill changes that keep landing in my lap keep me creatively challenged but as they keep occurring, I am getting fearful of mental fatigue. I was now in my early to mid-fifties and my body and psyche are starting to wish for more peace. How am I going to solve the financial issues of impending aging and retirement?

And of course, there is still my caregiving responsibility. It is absolutely critical that I continue to develop solutions for solving all of John's growing health issues. Gratefully, he is extremely self-sufficient. He can feed, bathe, and dress himself, keep himself busy with his life's purpose, and he is generally happy. My role at home is purely that of health care manager, therapy manager, housekeeper, grocery shopper, bill payer, cat management system, automobile management system, laundress, taxi service to doctors for John, and general manager. This sounds like the typical job description of every overwhelmed full-time parent. I guess I am not alone in my borderline despair.

LESSONS LEARNED

Despite my occasional internal doubt, I was making my "new kind of music" while I was teaching instead of being a composer and performer. In reality, I was too busy to notice the change. However since this new kind of music was so rewarding, I was able to let go of the pain of giving up my career as a performer and composer.

I liked to think of myself as a palm tree instead of an oak. The palm tree bends in the hurricane winds and is flexible. It withstands the storm. Although very strong, the oak breaks in the wind and the falling branches do damage to others. The incredible lesson I learned was to change and bend with the flow of what the Universe

> offered. I had to allow the paradigm shift. As long as I could accept a new and, as I learned, rewarding gift, then my new music glowed with as much glory as had my past career as a performer.

At the three year point of working for the technical college, I resigned my position to focus on managing the four real estate investment properties I had acquired during my teaching tenure when I had real income. These properties were my plan for financial security in my retirement years.

When I left that teaching job, I decided to get my Real Estate License in the State of California and move into that business again. I could be self-employed. I believed my previous experience as a REALTOR® in Florida, my organizational skills as a free-lance musician, and the freedom of working for myself would add the much needed quality of life for me. That was the good news. The bad news was that I got my license in February of 2007, just a few days before the real estate bubble burst in California, the United States, and eventually the entire world. I was one among millions of people for whom that economic crash caused enormous financial hardship. Both my budding real estate career and my real estate investments crashed simultaneously.

After two years of agonizing, I had to sell, below value, three of my investment properties because I could no longer support them. I also sold our personal home and John and I moved into a small apartment building I own.

☙

The Universe then provided the next amazing piece of the puzzle. This move created intense downsizing of "things" we own and has brought an even greater peace than I have ever imagined. In our new city, I found people of like mind and began taking meditation and yoga classes. I found a new spiritual home in this wonderful city. This peace allows me the time and space I need to learn and grow spiritually on so many levels. Because the real estate market is still struggling to recover, I have time to meditate, write, and become truly aware of my inner self: the real me.

I have now embraced the wisdom that my inner world does truly create my outer world. I am beginning to attract something different than what I thought I had always wanted. I now attract what I am. Since I live each day in peace and love, I attract more of the same. The Law of Attraction, which states that we attract the energy we put out into the Universe, rings true for me.

Caregiving is now extremely easy because my heart sings with the joy of being in service to someone else. When I sing, there is no burden. Each task gets lighter each day. Whatever needs to be done gets done as a part of my inner light, not because I have to do each task.

☙

Now, all the pieces of my life's puzzle are here on the table in front of me. All the fears of the initial trauma are pieces. All the agonizing tears of mourning the loss of my spouse and friend as he was are merely pieces. All the fatigue from years of assisting with therapy, changing careers, and the adding of yet more and more skills on my résumé were simply the paths that guided me to my personal shift. They mean little externally, for they are just pieces of the puzzle. Without them, I would not have been able to make the even larger shift that has brought me to live each new day with wisdom and gratitude.

The lessons I learned along the way are those that I needed to learn. I learned them by analyzing the situation at hand. I learned them by using the extensive resources around me. I learned them by reading the books listed in the resources appendix. I learned them because my brain is wired a certain way that is unique to me. Meditation is a skill I have adopted to bring additional peace to my soul. That peace clears the way so that I may learn more lessons. Most importantly I learned these lessons by making the choice to accept the paradigm shifts.

As I now assemble these pieces that have revealed themselves along the way, I have discovered a triumphant and beautiful picture of my life's purpose. All those pieces of my life—the skills I learned, the lessons I have been honored to receive and accept, all the paradigm shifts—these gifts from Spirit all led me in the direction of finding my new music.

I did not stop the music at all—I just found a new music of joy. My New Music, my passion, my purpose, is about being a Caregiver from a place of true and unconditional love. It is unconditional love for who I am, for John, for our life together, and for all of the Lessons Learned. It is about living in gratitude for all of the gifts given by the Universe. It is about experiencing the complex musical composition that unfolds anew each day. All of the notes of my song are resplendent as they dance on the musical staff paper where the title of the composition is Caregiver.

<u>That</u> is the **Joy In Caregiving.**

ख Namaste ख

Epilogue
Don't Stop Your Music

Although this book is about the journey through life of two professional musicians and composers, there is a higher intention for the title and theme of this saga. That intention is to share our journey to the knowledge that there are no rules, no promises and no guarantees that your life will be as you planned or as you want. However, the sweet result of our time together, learning and growing within our own sense of purpose has brought us to not only understanding, but also living unconditional love, joy, and peace each day. Our goal is to share our learning and growth with you.

At the beginning stage of our journey, John and I were merely reacting to a set of catastrophic medical emergencies. There was very little joy available, mainly because there was literally no time to see that it was there. Our days were drenched in the halting and disparate melody of survival. I know I was running on adrenaline most of the time. Although we chose our methodology of dealing with it well, and finding the solutions to do so, there were so many solutions to find. Each moment was flooded as if a discordant voice was spewing unsavory notes onto our manuscript paper. That paper was soggy with way too much black ink: a cacophony of disharmony.

The joy would appear later, much later. In hindsight, I know it also appeared subtly, but yet often unnoticed along the way. It is now making itself apparent in each word, each sentence that I share. Our purpose is to bring the spirit of hope to others who are stepping in this inky river of medical trauma by our gift to you: an example of how to seek the joy.

Your personal music may be that of tilling fields, working in clay, teaching others, delivering food to the tables of hungry patrons, building streets, or any other of millions of tasks that each of us does on a daily basis. It is your special music. We both played our own music, and if we can do it, so can you.

LESSONS LEARNED

Be flexible: bend with the wind of chance, accept the responsibility of choosing to live each moment, each day, to the best of your ability at that moment. Accept the paradigm shifts. Live by choice, by taking action, and be grateful for the opportunity to discover that everything can be an opportunity. If you are a parent, teach your children these concepts: it is the best gift you can give them.

Let the beauty of your music resonate within your soul in each moment of every day. Be alive: live your passion. Whatever you do, choose to do it well. Whatever happens to you throughout each day is merely a step on the path of discovery that allows you the opportunity to experience love, joy, and peace. Let that peace resonate through your soul and you will live in gratitude.

Life always intervenes in its own enigmatic way. Let it! Play your own music, don't stop. Sometimes the melodies changes, but keep playing, no matter what happens.

One final note—both John and I know from deep within our souls, that this book is the Happiest Accident of all. Every experience we had along the way—John's stroke, the fact that we are musicians, and our belief that we would be successful each day, has given us the lessons we learned. All of the lessons have empowered both John and me. It is all about our attitude and the choice we have made to choose joy. We live in gratitude for each lesson and each day.

The Happiest Accident is this: our lessons are gifts to us and they are now our gift to you. It is our hope that from reading our book, you will find the same Joy in Caregiving that we live each day.

Nancy Weckwerth

~Thank you for experiencing our story~

Everything Has Its Time

*The strongest winds wreak havoc
but die away with time.
The rain may last for weeks
but finally passes over.
Even the cosmos
will finally pass away.
Everything has its time.
Everything passes.*

*If we open ourselves to life
we become one with all we are
and with all we do.
Joy and sorrow become part
of just one wondrous whole.
Within this whole,
everything has its time.*

"The Caregiver's Tao Te Ching" by William and Nancy Martin.

Acknowledgements

It is with profound sincerity that I say thanks to everyone who assisted in the creation of this work. You gave me support and assisted with vision. You listened to my attempts and my successes. Then your gentle guidance helped me to be a better writer.

To John: you gave me the courage to begin. You have been the inspiration for the entire book. Without your sacrifices, none of this would have happened. Thank you for sharing the tears, the laughter, and the joy. Your amazingly positive attitude in the face of all of our challenges has kept me on track to the finish line. You have believed in me always. My most sincere gratitude goes out to you forever.

To Martha: for over the past twenty-five years, you have given John and me support and friendship on so many levels. I look forward to being your friend and giving back to you for the next quarter century or longer. Thank you for being with us on this amazing journey called life.

To Jayasri: thank you for your help as an editor and friend. You made me want to be a better writer and showed me how to accomplish that task.

To all of the Cheerleaders: Bill, Irene, Nancy, Susan, and other friends and family members, thank you for being a part of John's and my lives. Thank you for being the light at the end of so many dark days. You still give us hope and smiles.

To all of the Listeners: Lisa and Laurén. You listened as I read it aloud to you. I got to watch the reactions on your beautiful faces! Thank you for being the ears of all readers.

To Nancy Peterson, PhD, and Eli Engel, MD, PhD: thank you for stepping Foreword! Your professional insights into the science behind my words, and to who I am as a person and as an author, have added immensely to the quality of the work.

To all those who have written cover testimonials: William, Martha, Bill, Irene, and Susan, thank you for the gift of your insights. Your reaction to the book gives all future readers a reason to look within. Thank you to those of you who write testimonials printed within the book pages and website: you are the voice of all readers.

To everyone at Balboa Press, thank you for your guidance, patience, and vision.

To everyone at the Hay House Writer's Workshop: Reid, Nancy, and Marianne, you gave me the tools, knowledge, and encouragement to walk this path as a professional. In the two days at San Mateo in 2013, your words changed my life. Most importantly, I learned to honor the process and place myself in service. To all of the "writer" friends I made at the workshop, thank you for your continued advice and encouragement. Write Because You Have To!

Thank you to our many musician friends who made life possible for the first two years after the stroke. Special thanks to members of the Disneyland Band for your financial support and again to the many members of Local 47 for the donations at the fundraiser. Your support went way beyond financial: it made John's recovery possible. His recovery is the foundation for the entire book.

Thank you to "The Three Musketeers": Muriel, Marj, and Dorothy, for your love and support in so many ways. Here's hoping you're reading this book from the beyond. We miss you dearly.

Special thanks to Justin for having my back with our current society's propensity for trying to misinterpret the true intention of the book.

One additional thought—I have dealt with great writer's block at not being able to say "thank-you" appropriately while writing this section of the book. Today, I began Day 1 of the twenty-one day "Meditation Experience" with Oprah and Deepak online. The title of this series is "Manifesting Grace through Gratitude." I meditated with them for just a few minutes before I started writing. Immediately after, the words of gratitude began to flow. So thank you, to Oprah and Deepak and the many others who contribute inspirational messages via the Internet. Your powerful messages affect others in ways you may never know. This time, I can say thanks for specific guidance. The Happy Accidents keep appearing.

Appendix I

Resources for Caregivers and Survivors

Internet:

The **American Stroke Association** is a vast compendium of news and information for survivors of stroke. A visit here will guide you to countless other websites of useful information. http://www.strokeassociation.org/STROKEORG/ John Swan has been given the "Stroke Hero" award by the American Stroke Association.
The **Family Caregiver Allianc**e is a national organization that supports Caregivers in all situations with help, ideas, and information. http://www.caregiver.org

Books:

The list below contains my favorite "reads" for Caregivers. It is by no means complete. The ones included are those that offer what I believe are unique insights and great resources for Caregivers. Because these books have such complete resources themselves, I did not see a need to add a more extensive list here.

Some of these books may be in your local library or bookstore. If they are not, they will all be available on the Internet at Amazon.com or the publisher's website. Enough information to locate them is included with each book.

Books written by Stroke Survivors
Because of recent medical advances, survivors of stroke have attained more complete recovery. Their ability to document their healing, as a result, is very valuable.
My Stroke of Insight: A Brain Scientist's Personal Journey
Jill Bolte Taylor, 2006, Penguin Group
Author Jill Bolte Taylor, a brain scientist, had a massive stroke in 1996. Her book explains her awareness of the process of the stroke as it was occurring and of her own healing from her point of view as a scientist. This book

book is highly recommended reading for anyone caring for someone who has had a stroke. It gives insights into what the person is experiencing that makes the job of Caregiver a little less confusing, so that you can be more forgiving of your Survivor's condition.

You may also visit her TED talks on the Internet or via your Smart TV using the app "TED". Put her name in the Search field and you will find them.

My Stroke of Luck
Kirk Douglas, 2003, IT Books

This is a celebrity book, from the point of view of the stroke patient and how his life changed as a result of his stroke. Because of the celebrity focus on the survivor himself, I have included it in my resources because it is inspirational for everyone.

Books written for and by Caregivers: Resource Books

The value of these books is that I, as an author, do not need to spend time re-inventing the wheel. The books below contain countless resources for Caregivers.

And Thou Shalt Honor: The Caregiver's Companion

Beth Witrogen McLeod, editor, 2002, Wiland-Bell Productions

As the companion book to the PBS Special, "And Thou Shalt Honor", producers Harry Wiland and Dale Bell bring to light the challenges facing today's caregivers. This book is the most complete resource book that is easily accessible for everyone. The final section on Caring for the Caregiver gives great hints on how to take care of yourself, so you can take care of others.

The Good Caregiver: A One-of-a-Kind Compassionate Resource for Anyone Caring for an Aging Loved One

Robert L. Kane, M.D., 2011, Penguin Group

Written by a medical doctor, this book is an excellent resource for Caregivers in any situation. It provides extensive medical descriptions, definitions of terms, and an extensive list of support resources for the Caregiver.

Books written by Caregivers: Personal Caregiving Accounts

Showcasing the personal struggles of caring for a spouse or close family member, the books below are the closest in content to "Don't Stop the Music". They speak to the personal side of being a Caregiver.

The Caregiver's Tao Te Ching: Compassionate Caring For Your Loved Ones and Yourself

William and Nancy Martin, 2011, New World Library

This is the source book for all of the poetry quoted in the preceding chapters. It is full of beautiful support; both spiritual and personal for any Caregiver.

Following is the official notice of copyright permission to use the excerpts:

From the book The Caregiver's Tao Te Ching. Copyright © 2011 by William and Nancy Martin. Reprinted with permission of New World Library, Novato, CA. www.newworldlibrary.com.

Passages in Caregiving: Turning Chaos into Confidence

Gail Sheehy, May 2010, William Morrow

This is a superb book, exquisitely written by a top professional writer. Sheehy gives many options for solutions for Caregivers. Most of her suggestions involve hiring a lot of professional support people to assist the Caregiver. Her list of resources for Caregivers is extensive.

Books mentioned or referred to in the chapters of "Don't Stop the Music."

With great appreciation to the authors, the following books are philosophical or personal growth books that explain concepts mentioned in my book in greater detail. I owe the authors of these books for much of what I learned along my journey to "Finding the Joy in Caregiving".

A Return to Love: Reflections on the Principles of A Course in Miracles

Marianne Williamson, 1992, Harper Collins

Marianne is a well-known teacher and lecturer on "A Course in Miracles". This particular book explains the need for all of us to awaken to the concept of love-based emotions and live with them as opposed to living with fear-based emotions.

The Power of Now: A Guide to Spiritual Enlightenment

Eckhardt Tolle, 1999, New World Library

Contemporary philosopher, Eckhardt Tolle, skillfully introduces the concept of living in the "now" as opposed to living in the past or sitting around waiting for the future to happen. This concept brings the reader to a new appreciation for the joy that is occurring each moment of every day.

A New Earth: Awakening to your Life's Purpose

Eckhardt Tolle, 2008, Walker and Co.

Building upon the concepts introduced in "The Power of Now", Tolle expands upon the concept of living in the "now" to include releasing our personal ego as a means of letting go of personal and interpersonal conflict and suffering. This brings us to the inspirational point of being able to live a fulfilled life in whatever we do.

Excuses Begone!: How to Change Lifelong, Self-Defeating Thinking Habits

Wayne Dyer, 2009, Hay House

In this book, Dr. Dyer teaches us how to let go of life long habits and beliefs about ourselves that no longer serve us. It is this methodology and philosophy that allows each of us to move forward, accept the paradigm shifts, and live a joyous life.

Appendix II

John D. Swan's Biography, Discography, List of Publications and Unpublished Compositions

Musical Education and Training
1969-71 <u>University of Miami, School of Music</u>, Coral Gables, Florida.   Doctor of Musical Arts, Theory-Composition. (advisor, J. Clifton Williams)
1965-66 <u>Eastman School of Music</u>, Rochester, New York.   The Arrangers' Workshop.
1961-64 <u>Yale University School of Music</u>, New Haven Connecticut.   Master of Music, Trumpet Performance.
1960-61 <u>University of Toronto, Faculty of Music</u>, Toronto, Ontario, Canada.   Bachelor of Music Education.

1956-60 <u>The Royal Conservatory of Music Toronto</u>, Toronto, Ontario, Canada.   Associate of the Royal Conservatory of Music Toronto, (ARCT), Trumpet Pedagogy.
1959-61 Private Study, Schillinger System, Schenker Analysis.   Private Instructor: Myron Schaeffer, Toronto, Ontario, Canada.
1958-61 Private Study, Theory and Composition.   Private Instructor: Gordon Delamont, Toronto, Ontario, Canada.
1951-61 Private Study, Trumpet   Private Instructor: Donald Johnson, Toronto, Ontario, Canada.

Employment History

1986-February 12, 1991 Free-lance Trumpeter, Composer, Arranger, Musical Director.
   Los Angeles, California.
Career Highlights:
  Featured Trumpet Soloist:
  The Beverly Hills Unlisted Jazz Band, Buddy Collette Orchestra, The Incredible Shade Band at Universal Studio Tours, The Disneyland Band.
  Musical Director:
  Rising Winds, a 10-piece wind and percussion

ensemble.
Composer/Arranger:
Composed most of the repertoire for Rising Winds. Arranged material for the Buddy Collette Orchestra.

1986-88 **Assistant Professor of Music.**
California State University, Los Angeles.

1983-86 Free-lance Trumpeter, Composer, Arranger, Music Director.
Toronto, Ontario.
Career Highlights:
Featured Trumpet Soloist:
Mantovani Orchestra, Jim Galloway Orchestra on the "Toronto Alive" radio shows from the Sheraton Hotel, Howard Cable Orchestra at the opening of the "Toronto International Festival", Ontario Place, 1984.
Composer/Arranger:
Composed and performed "Papal Fanfare and Recessional" for Pope John Paul at St. Michael's Cathedral, Toronto, Ontario 9/14/84.
Arranged and performed "Granada" for Marco Valenti, on tour with the Mantovani Orchestra, 1985.
Musical Director:
The Old Mill Orchestra

1983-84 Concert Band Director.
Humber College of the Applied Arts and Sciences, Rexdale, Ontario, Canada.

1979-83 Faculty, Free-lance Trumpeter, Composer, Arranger, Music Director. South Florida.
Assistant Professor of Music.
Florida Atlantic University, Boca Raton, Florida.
Career Highlights:
Principal trumpet:
The Greater Palm Beach Symphony Orchestra, Palm Beach, Florida.
Free-lance Trumpeter, Composer, Arranger.
Miami, Fort Lauderdale, and Palm Beach, Florida.
Musical Director:
The Brass Ring, The Swing Machine, Mixed Bag, Fanfara.
Created **Trombacor Music**, a music publishing company in conjunction with Nancy Weckwerth.

1978-79 **Assistant Professor of Music.**
University of Western Ontario, London, Ontario, Canada.

1976-78 **Co-Principal Trumpet.**
Fort Lauderdale Symphony, Fort Lauderdale, Florida.

1975-76 **Master Teacher.** Humber College of the Applied Arts and Sciences, Rexdale Ontario.
1973-75 **Assistant Professor of Music.** Florida International University, Miami, Florida
1972-73 **Free-lance Trumpeter.** Miami, Florida.
1969-71 **Doctoral Candidate.** University of Miami, Coral Gables, Florida.
1965-72 **Assistant Professor of Music.** University of British Columbia, Vancouver, British Columbia, Canada
1963-65 **Chairman: Music Department.** Iolani School, Honolulu, Hawaii. **Principal Trumpet.** Honolulu Symphony, Honolulu, Hawaii.
Awards
1963 **Canada Council Grant** and **Yale Alumni of Canada Scholarship** To attend Yale University School of Music, New Haven, Connecticut 1965 **The Duke Ellington Scholarship** To attend Eastman School of Music 2014 **"Stroke Hero"** The American Stroke Association

Discography Highlights

Erny's Summer Jazz Festival: Live From Erny's, 1981 Spinnster Records sp0001, jazz trumpet performer and arranger with Chubby and Duffy Jackson

    https://www.youtube.com/watch?v=cTor-yIRFak
    https://www.youtube.com/watch?v=Kcm3dEAqw68

Once in a While, 1982 Spinnster Records sp0002, jazz trumpet performer with Pete Minger and Eddie Higgins. Nancy Weckwerth performed on one track on this album.

Live at El Camino College, 2006, with the Buddy Collette Big Band. Arranger.

Publications – Music

Columbia Pictures Publications, Hialeah, Florida

    Compositions:

Toro Misterioso, 1979 (trumpet solo with concert band)

    Arrangements: 1977-79

Christmas Medley, (brass quintet)

Brick House (marching band)

Sir Duke (brass quintet and woodwind quintet)

Star Wars (brass quintet and woodwind quintet)

Still (brass quintet and woodwind quintet)

Thank You for Being a Friend (marching band)

You Light Up My Life (brass quintet and woodwind quintet)
We Will Rock You (marching band)
Kendor Music, Delevan, New York
Golden Sands, 1973 (concert band)
Ludwig Music Publishing Co., Cleveland, Ohio
Hard Sock Dance, 1977 (trumpet and piano)
Trombacor Music, Los Angeles, California
Compositions: 1968-1990
And In The Center Ring (trombone solo with brass ensemble)
A Raggy Boogaloo (trombone solo with brass ensemble and rhythm section)
B.Q. Blues (brass quintet)
Ballad for Trumpet (brass ensemble and rhythm section)
Blues and Ballads (8 French horns)
B.Q. Blues (brass ensemble and rhythm section)
Ceremonial Suite (brass quintet wedding music co-composed with Nancy Weckwerth)
Chaconne and Variations (brass quintet)
Chase Music (brass ensemble)
Chorale and Variants (brass trio)
Concert Piece for Horn and Winds (horn and wind ensemble)
Dance Suite #1 (brass quintet)
Dance Suite #2 (brass quintet)
Divertimento (brass quartet)

Exotica (horn solo with brass quintet)
Fanfare (brass ensemble)
Fanfare and Rondo (brass choir)
Functional Fanfares (trumpet duets)
Flugel Dance (brass ensemble)
Marching Mutes (brass trio)
Opener (brass ensemble)
Papal Fanfare and Recessional (brass choir)
Petit Rondeau de Concert (horn solo with brass ensemble)
Piccolo Polka (brass ensemble)
Pop (brass ensemble)
Sonata for Horn (horn and piano)
Thonk! Thonk! (tuba solo with brass quintet)
Trombacor Suite(trumpet and horn duets co-composed with Nancy Weckwerth)
Variations (brass quartet)

Arrangements: 1983-1990

Air on the G String – Bach (brass quintet)
Allegro for Piccolo Trumpets – Torelli (brass ensemble)
Andante Cantabile – Tchaikovsky (brass ensemble)
Aragonaise from Le Cid – Massenet (brass quintet)
Auld Lang Syne – Burns (brass ensemble)
Carmen Medley – Bizet (brass trio)
Fantasy on Hava Nagila – traditional (brass quintet)
March of the Sardar – Ivanov (brass ensemble)

Polonaise Opus 40 #1 – Chopin (brass quintet)
Pop (Goes the Weasel) – traditional (brass ensemble)
Romanza – Mozart (brass ensemble)
School Concert Brass Ensembles – (a collection of works for brass ensemble)
Sonata for Trumpet – Purcell (brass ensemble)
Sonatina – Diabelli (brass trio)
The Saints – traditional (brass ensemble)

Publications – Prose

A Practice Routine for Brass Players, 1983, Trombacor Music, Los Angeles, California
The Way I See It, vol. 7, #3, 1973, NAJE Educator
Varese's Octandre as a Source Piece for Three Twentieth Century Compositional Procedures, vol.1 #2, 1972, CAUSM Journal

Unpublished Works

Orchestra
  Leharjinn, 1985, ballet, co-composed with Nancy Weckwerth (composed for the International Ballet Composition Competition, Geneva, Switzerland.)
Rising Winds 1986-1991 (Ten–piece Wind Ensemble of jazz and classical performers)
  Arrangements:
  Anything Goes Medley (Cole Porter)
  Airegin (Sonny Rollins)

How Long Has This Been Going On (George Gershwin)
Goe From My Window (John Munday)
Prelude To A Kiss (Duke Ellington)

Original Compositions:
A Day In My Life
Antithetical Musings
Ballade and Courante
Concert Piece for Horn and Winds
Dodecaphonics
Dream Lover
Eccentric Dances
Enigma
Exotic Lands
Flutterbye
Folding My Tent
Hommage to R.W.
Mechanics
Midwinter 1986
Overture to a Tiny Tempest
Resolved
Riding the Wave
Rondo
Symphony #1
Symphony #2
Tango for Snakes
Too Many Variations

Travelogue
Very Unsettling
1945 Suite

Chamber Music (1968-1979)
A Diverting Piece (brass quartet and rhythm section)
Brass Quartet
Chorale and Variants for Brass Trio
Fantasy For Brass Quintet
String Quartet
Variations on S.G.B. (trumpet, alto saxophone, cello, and percussion)
Woodwind Quintet

Concert Band 1969-1987
Colours (Composed as partial requirement for the Doctor of Musical Arts, University of Miami)
Fantasy on the British Grenadiers (Composed for the 7th Regiment Royal Canadian Artillery Band in Toronto, Ontario, Canada)
Largo and Dance
Sail Away (Composed for the Royal Canadian Navy March Competition)

Small Jazz Band 1979-1983 (trumpet, saxophone, and rhythm section)
A Little Humour There
At It Again
(Recorded on "Live At Erny's", Spinnster Records SP0001)

Four Black Bugs
Gay Old Vienna
Holy Men Walking
Jerome's Kernels
Morning Walk
Onward for Lust and Greed
'Orrid 'Arry
Pas De Nom
R.B. Influence
Requiem
Six to Five
Solid Jackson Greetings Gate
Sophistry
Triad
Who Parked the Car?

Solo Instruments and Piano 1968-1974
Recipes (voice and piano)
Trumpet Sonata (trumpet and piano)

Solo Instruments and Ensembles 1972-1980
Concert Piece for Trumpet and Jazz Band
Fiesta (trumpet and band)
Rhapsody for French Horn and Wind Ensemble
Variants for Trombone and Band
Trumpet Concerto (trumpet and strings)

Stage Band 1965-1975
Jazz Canadiana Suite (Commissioned by CBC Radio, Vancouver. 2 trumpets, 2 saxophones,

trombone, string quartet, rhythm section and auxiliary percussion.)
Mixed Bag
Seconds
Drone

Miscellaneous Compositions 1966
Miss Rosie (Film Score for clarinet, piano, and percussion)

Visit John on facebook at:
https://www.facebook.com/pages/Dont-Stop-the-Music-John-D-Swan/260829299098?ref=hl

or, if the following link is clickable

Don't Stop the Music: Finding the Joy in Caregiving

Appendix III

Glossary and Internet Resources

For those interested in exploring the Internet for more information on terms and topics mentioned in the book, the Internet addresses are included below.

Medically related terms
Aphasia (including Broca's Aphasia)
    http://www.strokeassociation.org/STROKEORG/LifeAfterStroke/RegainingIndependence/CommunicationChallenges/Types-of-Aphasia_UCM_310096_Article.jsp
Fibromuscular dysplasia
    http://my.clevelandclinic.org/heart/disorders/vascular/fibromuscular_dysplasia.aspx
Glaucoma
    http://www.mayoclinic.com/health/glaucoma/DS00283
Mohs Surgery Technique
    http://www.skincancer.org/skin-cancer-information/mohs-surgery
Neurologist
    http://en.wikipedia.org/wiki/Neurologist
Physicians' Desk Reference (PDR)
    http://www.pdr.net/
Skin Cancer
    http://www.skincancer.org/skin-cancer-information/squamous-cell-carcinoma
Stroke
    http://en.wikipedia.org/wiki/Stroke

General Terms
Americans With Disabilities Act (ADA) was enacted into law in 1990.
http://www.ada.gov
Insight Seminars
http://www.insightseminars.org
Kübler Ross Model
https://en.wikipedia.org/wiki/Kübler-Ross_model
Raku Firing Technique
http://ceramicartsdaily.org/category/firing-techniques/raku-firing-techniques/

Colleges, Universities, and other Educational Institutions
Concordia College
http://www.concordiacollege.edu/
Florida Atlantic University
http://www.fau.edu/
Iolani School
http://www.iolani.org/
Royal Conservatory of Toronto
https://examinations.rcmusic.ca/
University of British Columbia
http://www.ubc.ca/
University of Miami
https://www.miami.edu/
University of Southern California
http://www.usc.edu
University of Toronto
http://www.utoronto.ca/
University of Western Ontario
http://www.uwo.ca/
University of Wisconsin – Eau Claire
http://www.uwec.edu
Yale University
http://www.yale.edu

Musical Organizations
Bach Corporation
   http://www.bachbrass.com/
Hawaii Symphony
   http://hawaiisymphonyorchestra.org/
Mantovani Orchestra
   http://www.themantovaniorchestra.com/

Index

A

advocate xi, 127, 201, 202, 203, 205, 209, 210, 211, 215
airport 189, 190, 191, 195
airports 188
Americans with Disabilities Act 188
Apraxia 250, 251
attitude xiv, xvii, xviii, xxx, xxxi, xxxii, xxxiii, xxxiv, 18, 36, 62, 63, 65, 67, 71, 73, 98, 112, 129, 130, 141, 161, 245, 251, 283, 285

B

balance 25, 36, 37, 38, 39, 43, 44, 53, 54, 55, 56, 63, 121, 133, 143

brain damage 7, 21, 22, 61, 66, 104, 114, 119, 120, 121, 123, 124, 129, 139, 179, 247
Brocas Aphasia ix, x, xi, 66, 149

C

Caregiver vii, xiii, xiv, xv, xvi, xvii, xxii, xxiii, xxxvi, 10, 14, 15, 18, 25, 34, 35, 50, 51, 54, 56, 63, 75, 76, 77, 82, 86, 92, 94, 96, 97, 99, 110, 117, 120, 121, 122, 123, 124, 126, 130, 133, 137, 138, 139, 140, 141, 142, 143, 145, 147, 148, 160, 161, 162, 163, 164, 169, 173, 176, 177, 178, 194, 196, 198, 199, 200, 202, 205, 209, 210, 211, 214, 215, 216, 220, 224, 226, 227, 234, 240, 241, 242, 243, 247, 251, 254,

257, 258, 262, 263, 267,
  279, 284, 289, 291, 292, 293
Caregivers Tao Te Ching xxiii,
  xxxvi, 15, 35, 56, 75, 99,
  126, 145, 164, 176, 199, 216,
  234, 292
Cerebral Vascular Accident
  xxxiii, 5, 100
Chinese Acupuncturist 157
choice xxx, xxxi, xxxiii, xxxiv,
  xxxv, 7, 27, 28, 32, 48, 61,
  63, 89, 90, 117, 130, 136,
  158, 167, 282
CHOICE 116
compassion 13, 17, 84, 115, 125,
  172, 175
CVA 59, 63, 66, 100, 104, 113,
  129, 131, 158, 246, 248.
  See cerebral vascular
  accident

F

fear-based 31, 32, 43, 55, 91
Fibro-muscular Dysplasia 101
Forgiveness 165, 174, 175

G

gig 1, 77, 78, 166
glaucoma 109, 211, 213, 311

gratitude xvii, xviii, xxx, xxxiii,
  xxxiv, 28, 36, 38, 63, 73, 74,
  90, 91, 98, 128, 144, 173,
  230, 233, 247, 278, 283,
  285, 288

H

Happy Accident 57, 58, 59, 61,
  64, 66, 68, 72, 74
health insurance 2, 25, 38, 39,
  40, 53, 54, 70, 87, 89, 90,
  101, 103, 161, 206, 266
HMO 41, 42, 53, 101, 103, 207

I

Insight Seminars 270
insurance company 4, 29, 39, 40,
  41, 42, 43, 44, 46, 47, 49,
  53, 86, 103, 153
Intensive Care 48, 49, 50

J

Joy in Caregiving 215

L

Law of Attraction xxxi, 277
LESSON LEARNED 31, 33,
  142, 188, 190, 266

LESSONS LEARNED 10, 28,
　　46, 52, 54, 90, 93, 108, 121,
　　137, 194, 214, 263, 275
loneliness 168, 169, 179, 185
love-based 18, 31, 32, 33, 34, 36,
　　52, 55, 91, 215

M

Mohs 109, 110
mourning 217, 218, 224, 225,
　　227, 228, 233, 278

N

NDT 70, 136
neuroplasticity 155

O

occupational therapy 132, 208
OT 69, 132, 133, 135, 207, 209.
　　See occupational therapy

P

paradigm shift 18, 31, 33, 34, 86,
　　90, 97, 120, 121, 124, 125,
　　145, 175, 222, 232, 240,
　　259, 262, 267, 276
Paradigm Shift 16, 17, 33, 219
Paradigm Shifts 19
PCP 60, 61

physical therapy 11, 105, 135,
　　143, 208
PPO 54, 266. *See* Preferred
　　Provider Oranization
pre-existing condition 53, 263
Preferred Provider
　　Organization 54
Primary Care Physician 101
P.T. *See* Physical Therapy

R

Rehabilitation Unit 11, 29, 105
Rehab Unit 12, 105, 132

S

Skilled Nursing Facility 12, 28,
　　40, 70, 166, 204
SNF 12, 29, 41, 133, 136,
　　156, 166, 205, 206, 207.
　　See Skilled Nursing
　　Facility
Solution 18, 108
Solutions 45, 51, 83, 111, 133,
　　135, 205, 210, 251
Speech Therapist 154
speech therapy 63, 64, 104, 127,
　　155, 156, 161, 207, 208
Spirit xxxiv, 34, 258, 279

spiritual 19, 28, 31, 34, 37, 55, 56, 227, 259, 267, 277

subway car 16, 17

surgery 43, 47, 48, 49, 50, 109, 110, 212, 311

T

The Man in the Mall 160

The Skilled Nursing Facility Saga 204

The Toronto Adventure 190

Trombacor Music 1, 79, 230, 238

U

Universe xxxi, xxxiii, xxxiv, 13, 52, 53, 69, 72, 73, 98, 168, 184, 194, 197, 241, 275, 277

V

victim mentality xxxi, xxxii, xxxiii

W

wheelchair 25, 26, 50, 71, 84, 133, 168, 169, 187, 188, 189, 190, 191, 192, 195, 202, 225, 253

William Churchill 148

About the Cover

The background images of music on the front and back cover of the book are the first and last pages of a composition written by John D. Swan. It is shown in Dr. Swan's handwriting. The wheelchair is a photograph of his personal wheelchair, with special effects created by the photographer. The trumpet is a photo of one of John's current trumpets.

All cover photography by Bev Widney Photography. Glendora, California.

All internal photography by David Field, Photographer. Toronto, Ontario, Canada.

The cover concept was designed by the author, Nancy Weckwerth.

About the Author

Nancy Weckwerth holds the Master of Music degree in Performance, the Bachelor of Music degree in Music Education, and the Certificate in Composition for the Music Industry. She has over 25 published musical compositions and arrangements. In addition, she has 3 prose articles published in professional music Journals.

She currently works as a REALTOR® in Southern California.

Her hobbies include making pottery and jewelry. Ms. Weckwerth volunteers regularly as a Foster MomKat for abandoned kittens, working with several non-profit pet adoption agencies.

Visit her websites: http://www.dontstopthemusic.co
http://www.nancyweckwerth.com
Nancy on facebook:
https://www.facebook.com/nancy.weckwerth.9

pp. 178-179 — List to stay at home alone